In God We Trust:
Everyone Else Pays Cash*

Today's Decisions That Will Impact Your Business Tomorrow

3rd Edition

Gene Marks

Quicker! Better! Wiser!
Publications
Bala Cynwyd, PA

*with credit to the great Jean Shepherd

ISBN: 1451589247
EAN: 9781451589245

Interior images pages 45, 89, 121 © Slavoljub Pantelic; page 1 © Fixer00; page 177 © Mmaxer; page 249 © Vasabii; page 281 © Mahesh Patil
All images used under 2013 license from Shutterstock.com

Gene's previous books include the #1 Amazon Small Business Best Seller *The Streetwise Small Business Book of Lists* (Adams Media), *The Small Business Desk Reference* (Alpha Books), *Outfoxing The Small Business Owner - Crafty Techniques for Creating a Profitable Relationship* (Adams Media) and *The Complete Idiot's Guide To Successful Outsourcing* (Alpha Books).

Unless otherwise noted, articles reprinted from Forbes Magazine, Inc. com, the Huffington Post and American City Business Journals by special permission, copyrights © 2007-2013.

Articles on pages 30, 34, 178, 250-260, 282, and 289-295 reprinted from Bloomberg Business Week by special permission, copyright © 2007-2013 by Bloomberg L.P.

The characters and examples in this book are based mostly on real individuals and companies and are used for illustration purposes only. In some cases the names have been changed.

Many of the designations used by manufacturers and sellers to distinguish their products are claimed as trademarks. Where those designations appear in this book and the author was aware of a trademark claim, the designations have been printed with initial capital letters.

Acknowledgements

Many people support my research, writing and business activities. The key people I want to thank are: Corey Babka, Jen Deslaurier, Maria Greendyk, Justin Hill, Alexis James, Caryn Maenza, Geri Rizzuto, Susan Vestal, Susan Weeks.

In God We Trust: Everyone Else Pays Cash

Generating Leads for Tomorrow's Business

Ways To Increase Revenues Today and in the Future

Getting More Production From Your People

Keeping Expenses In Line Now To Free Up Cash Later

Managing Your Cash Flow Over Time

Technology Trends That You Must Follow To Stay Competitive

The Economy, The World....Your Business

Conclusion

Introduction

We run businesses. And we have responsibilities. People rely on us. Our employees. Our customers. Our suppliers. Our partners. Our families. It is not our job to just make payroll. In fact if you're concerned about making next week's payroll, this book isn't for you.

This book is for the owner and manager working in an established business that is looking forward. He (or she) isn't thinking about next week or next month. This person is looking out over the next few years.

Because if you're not generating a sufficient number of leads today you're not going to be able to fund your company tomorrow. If you're not thinking all the time about ways to increase revenues and grow your business then there probably won't be any business some day in the future. If you think that your employees are as happy and productive as they'll ever be then this is where you'll always be. If you're not always wondering about ways to reduce overhead and lower your costs then someday someone is going to come along and outthink you. If you're not managing your cash the right way today then you'll be missing a bunch of it when you'll one day really need it.

If you're not keeping up with technology then you're going to fall behind. And if you're not keeping up with what's going on in the world around you, the political environment and economic cycles then how will you be able to manage in the dark? What will you do when interest rises or inflation jumps?

How does the Fed impact your business? How can the nation's budget deficit potentially cripple you? What are you doing today to minimize your taxes a few years from now?

This is why we make the BIG bucks, right? We're supposed to be navigating the ship, looking ahead, watching the horizon for potential storm clouds and reacting appropriately to ensure that we stay on course.

We may believe in God, we may not. But, as business people, we definitely believe in cash. How to make it now and what we need to be doing to continue making it in the future. So here's a few ideas from some very smart business people I know.

And that's because I've learned a lot from smart business people. People who've taught me things about billing and collecting. Costing jobs. Using technology correctly. The lessons from many experts are here: managers, owners, CEOs. And of course, Paris Hilton.

And because of them I'm squeezing more profits from my company. I'm closing a few more sales. I'm keeping a few more customers happy. I'm motivating and getting production from my people. I'm managing my cash better and have a better understanding of the economy.

I'm a business owner and my ten person company is making money. This book explains how I've learned to do things a little quicker, better and wiser. Maybe some day I can be someone's BFF too. Right, Paris?

Generating Leads

For Tomorrow's Business

It Really Is Location, Location, Location

I grew up in a large dual-apartment complex outside of Philadelphia. And I remember Mike The Greek and Sam The Pharmacist very well. Mike sold me cigarettes. Sam sold me porn. I was in middle school. Great business people, both.

Mike The Greek ran a small grocery store in the basement of the complex. His store was there when I was born (or so I was told) and was still there when I was kicked out of my home after college. Mike, an immigrant who spoke with a thick accent and had arms the size of Rosie O'Donnell's ran the pre-cursor to today's 7-Eleven convenience store. He sold all the essentials, like milk, bread and Marlboros. He had a little deli in the back for sandwiches, too, where you could get bologna, salami and all the other delicious lunch meats that were eaten guilt-free in the '70s.

Sam's pharmacy, located just a few feet away from Mike The Greek's store, outstayed me as well. Sam made his living selling Darvon, Dexatrim and Valium to the stay-at-home moms and aging WW2 veterans that made up most of the tenant population. And his rack of Playboys, Hustlers and Oui magazines were a dream for any young adolescent like myself, especially if I could scare up the two bucks necessary to purchase a copy for (wink, wink) my dad. Ah, good times. Good times.

These guys ran small, but profitable businesses. Businesses that bought them houses, cars and paid for their kids' college educations. Sure, the money came from overly prescribed drugs, cancer-causing lunchmeats and "men's magazines". But it was the '70s, man. It was all cool. And after many years Mike The Greek and Sam The Pharmacist sold their shops and retired. Other than the sideburns, mustaches and cowboy boots, these men were not unlike many business owners I know today.

They were experts at marketing. And they didn't even know it.

Neither employed marketing firms or consultants. They never bought into mass mailing campaigns or hired telemarketers. They didn't waste money on advertising, save for a flier or two taped up in the building's elevators or a notice tacked on to the bulletin board.

They just picked their location wisely and served their community well.

They went to where their customers lived. They offered products with fair prices and good services. And they were in our face all the time. Their shops, located just a few yards down the hall from the complex's mailroom, were visited by just about every tenant every day. The few commercial firms that also rented space in the building bought sandwiches and toiletries from them. Visitors to the building often stopped by to purchase a paper or a can of Tab before leaving. It was convenient. And it made sense.

Look around and you'll see other smart business people doing the same. Things haven't changed much. I see CPAs and attorneys with offices in downtown buildings where half the tenants just happen to be their clients, too. I see an optician on the ground floor of another office building who sells most of her glasses and contact lenses to tenants that walk by her shop every day. I see a computer guy who opened up a little storefront on main street and services the many small businesses and retail shops within a half mile away. I see my client who manufactures electro-magnetic testing machines for the military and who is located on the footsteps of a large Air Force base. I see my friend who sells financial services software and keeps offices near Wall Street.

Location really does count. Because even in this big old world of billions of people most businesses still just serve their immediate communities. Mike the Greek and Sam the Pharmacist served the community inside the apartment complex. Where's your community? How far away are they? Should you be closer?

Sometimes marketing gets too complicated. Coca-Cola can have a complicated marketing plan. Many business people don't need to be so complicated. Picking a spot to do business, close to customers, often is the best marketing one needs to do.

90210 Meets 'Twilight'

Jason hates high school kids.

He hates the way they dress, with their baggy pants and torn clothing. He hates their nose rings, tattoos and pierced intestines. He hates their new secret language that they use to communicate with each other over cell phones and computers. He hates Urban Dictionary, Twitter and Facebook. And he hates that fact that an 18-year-old's vote counts exactly the same as his.

So why does he employ high school kids? "Because they're cheap," he says with a smile. "And they help me sell my products."

They do this by not meeting a single customer or prospective customer. In fact, the high school kids he employs are not even allowed to speak to a customer or prospective customer. But they still significantly contribute to Jason's revenue.

They telemarket. After hours. "Oh, and they're cheap," Jason said. "Did I mention that?"

Jason knows that high school kids are different. Have you ever seen "Scarred" on MTV? Have you ever listened to Flo Rida? Have you ever suffered through an episode of "Gossip Girl?" There is a certain part of the brain that needs to be switched off to enjoy these things. High school kids are one step ahead of this. They just keep it switched off.

But Jason knows that most high school kids can read. And, with a little practice, they can even sound somewhat human on the phone. "And they're cheap, too," said Jason.

So every night he has two high schoolers come into his office. And they make calls from a script.

They call customers. They call prospective customers. And here's the thing: Jason forbids them to speak to a human being. "Messages only," he warns. "If a human being picks up the phone, then hang up and move on." The last thing Jason needs is for one of these high schoolers to engage in a conversation. That's a guaranteed way to put himself out of business.

So they leave messages from a script he prepares. Sometimes the message is about a new product that he's offering. Or a special deal on a product he wants to move. Sometimes, especially to customers, it's a message checking in and asking if they'd like to order more of a product they bought in the past. Sometimes it's just a message to wish the customer a happy birthday or seasons greetings. It's a short voice mail, no longer than 20 seconds.

"Most people I know listen to their voice-mail messages, even if it's for the first five or 10 seconds," Jason said. "So in that time, I can get in a little hello and mention of my company."

Telemarketing is just one of the ways that Jason uses to keep in front of his current and prospective customers. He uses this method along with direct mail and e-mail. It's all part of his marketing. He doesn't expect a customer to immediately call back and place a big order, just because a high school kid left a voice mail. But, over time, when that customer has the need, Jason hopes that he'll be thought of first. Because he's checking in once in a while. Leaving messages. Keeping in touch.

"And it's cheap," Jason said. OK, he's got a point there.

High school kids can be had for under $10 an hour, a few hundred cans of Red Bull and a high-speed Internet connection so they can keep i-chatting. In the scheme of marketing expenses, it isn't much.

Jason's a smart manager. He knows that marketing takes a consistent approach. He knows that it's all about the touch, and how many times he can touch. And he finds inexpensive ways to keep his company's name in front of the potential audience. Even if it involves enduring a few high schoolers while they make calls after hours. It's effective. And most importantly? Well, you heard Jason about how much they cost.

Adada Muhammadu Needs Some List Advice

I feel really sorry for Mr. Adada Muhammadu.

A business owner, he's apparently suffering a great deal of tragedy in his home country of Nigeria and is looking for someone to safeguard $30 million that he holds in his bank account. Apparently, he recently inherited this amount from a wealthy relative and needs to get it out of his country as soon as possible. Naturally, he e-mailed me and asked if I could help for a 10 percent fee.

I'm thinking it over. It's a tough call.

I'm a busy guy with lots to do. I just don't have the time to e-mail him my bank account information and Social Security number, let alone travel to Nigeria, like he asks, to finalize arrangements. I'm supposed to take my daughter to a swim meet next week and I promised my wife I'd clean out the garage.

Otherwise I'd be good to go.

I'm just not a good candidate for him at this time. I wish he hadn't wasted his efforts on me. I guess my name came up on the list he purchased of smart, handsome men with hot wives. And I feel bad that he's throwing his money away on a list that he purchased that is not working out. So next time, Mr. Muhammadu, I have some advice for you.

For starters, I know a lot of good database companies that sell marketing lists.

Don't worry, Mr. Muhammadu. I don't agree with those few critics who theorize that the information these companies have is "throw-away" and out of date. This may be true in some cases, but I do know that there are many good database companies that invest in quality research and put a lot of emphasis on the integrity of the data they sell.

Even so, Mr. Muhammadu, you're going to need to be very careful when you buy your next list. Your e-mail reached me, but even with the best database companies around, my experience is that at least 50 percent of the contact info on a typical list is bad. A list can cost about $1 per name, so if you're going to drop $5,000-$10,000 (and many database companies have a minimum purchase in that range) you can expect thousands of e-mails and just as many letters to come bouncing back. The cost of this could significantly bite into the $30 million you're trying to transfer.

Here's one thing you may want to consider: The U.S. Postal Service offers something called the National Deliverability Index. An NDI score indicates how accurately the addresses in a mailing list match the latest address data maintained by the U.S. Postal Service. Mailing lists are matched using automated address verification programs. A good database company, if asked, will disclose this index to you. It's a way that the U.S. Post Office can help you and all your friends in Nigeria.

If you need to purchase another list of Americans who are willing to give up their private financial information in order to help you with your $30 million transfer, first try World Wrestling Entertainment - they may have plenty of good prospects for you. But be sure to get a sample first. Many list companies will send you 10 or 15 names for you to validate. And then when you ultimately get your list, make sure it's in a format where you can easily import it into a database or computer program, and is compatible with Microsoft Excel, or in text format that can be imported. Once imported, you've got to make sure you're doing the right follow-ups too.

Because that's one thing I noticed you didn't do very well, Mr. Muhammadu: Your follow-up was pretty lame. I just got one lousy e-mail from you. I realize I'm a little too busy right now, but a couple more e-mails or even a letter (especially when you write them so endearingly in all caps with those catchy misspellings) might have further enticed me to pay more attention to your plight.

I'm not so crazy about the e-mail thing, either, Mr. Muhammadu. Many database companies lack good e-mail information. And I'm not sure how many people opted in to receive your e-mail, even as enticing as it seems to be. The last thing you want is someone reporting you to the Nigerian Federal Trade Commission or putting you on some kind of blacklist. How then would you ever transfer your $30 million? Think, Mr. Muhammadu, think! Maybe in future you can use this data for regular direct mailing and telemarketing in addition to some e-mailing.

Here's an even better option: Instead of buying your list from a database company or from the WWE, you might want to either buy or rent from a magazine or trade publication. They're a little more expensive and some of them are only for limited use. However, I've had great success when I buy or rent lists from industry publications, because their list of subscribers is updated. In future you may want to try respected trade periodicals, like Architects With No Brains Digest or the popular Morons Weekly. Here you may find a very targeted population of American subscribers who, I bet, would be very interested in your plight.

I've met some smart managers who avoid buying lists altogether. They find that after spending the five or ten grand, and throwing out 50 percent of the data, they're spending even more time cleaning up what's left.

I talked to one such guy, a friend of mine in Kenya named Ngobe Ngayaka, and he said that when he sends e-mails to Americans asking to transfer his millions of dollars, he pays local high school students an hourly wage to dig up names from the Internet.

"Sure, my list of dumb Americans is smaller than if we would purchase a list," he said to me over a delicious bowl of ugali one night. "But my high school students are quite good at finding fools and idiots from your country from online sites. And at the hourly wage I pay them, I get much better data for the investment." Ngobe and I always poke fun at each other - I like to make fun of his country's soccer team. He makes jokes about my country's entire adult population. Oh, we just laugh and laugh.

But enough kidding around.

Mr. Muhammadu, I realize that you are trying to transfer a serious amount of money out of your country before you lose it. You desperately need our help. If anyone reading this is interested, please contact him - and have your banking and personal credit information available. Let someone come forward and live up to the reputation we Americans have around Nigeria, Kenya and the rest of the world.

Umm... Bob? Why the Brochure?

Recently I got a slick marketing brochure in the mail from Bob, my landscaper. It advertised all the great things Bob's company can do for me. OK, OK, yes, I have a landscaper. And yes, I'm lazy. But let's not get my wife all riled up. This is not about my laziness. It's about Bob's stupid attempt at marketing using a stupid marketing brochure. No smart manager would waste his time doing this.

First of all, the guy's a landscaper. I think he's got about 40 or so employees during his busiest season. Creating a professional marketing brochure is expensive. He must have hired a firm to do this. Printing it up costs a lot. Postage costs a lot. Putting together a list (or even buying one, which is probably what he did) costs a lot. Paying someone in his office or a mail-house to send out the piece costs a lot.

The whole exercise costs a lot. Too much. Landscapers, and similar small businesses that cater to homes and consumers shouldn't be spending this kind of money unless it's really part of a continuous marketing effort that has defined objectives. Brochures and marketing pieces can be effective. But managers know that a one-off mailing like Bob's isn't going to accomplish much.

Why am I receiving this stupid brochure anyway? The guy's already my landscaper. His brochure tells me all the great services that his firm can do, like planting bushes and cleaning up yards and seeding new gardens. Well duh ... isn't that what landscapers do?

How stupid is this? I'm already a customer of his. Didn't we all learn in Business 101 that it's more profitable to generate revenue from your existing customers than to try to create new business from new customers? Sending me this brochure isn't going to do it. How naïve. And how (gasp) environmentally unfriendly too! I threw out the brochure as soon as I got it. And notified the Democratic Party, too.

So what should my landscaper friend be doing to get more business from me? It's not that hard.

First, Bob fires his marketing firm. Then he sits down and makes a list of the top 15 things he knows that his customers like to do to their homes and gardens. He includes in this list some great ideas of his own. Then he gives this list to each crew leader.

Each week, when out doing his work, the crew leader checks his list and identifies opportunities. Then he makes it a point to find me. And he says this:

"We noticed that there's an excessive amount of dog poopiwawa on your lawn. We can create a lot of fertilizer from it to nurture a new garden of polka-dot flowers. It would be very nice."

And I would say "Gosh, Mr. Crew Leader, that sounds like an excellent idea. Please have your men turn my dog's poopiwawa into beauty." And there you go.

And hey, Bob, why not give your crew leader and his hard working team a few extra bucks when he sells these new services. Incentive. Motivation. Involvement. Sounds like one of the posters hanging in your office, right?

Want another crazy idea? OK, here it is: Call me.

"Hello Mr. Marks, it's Bob, the owner of Bob's Landscaping Services. Other than the time you stiffed me on that one spring cleanup, you've been a super customer of ours.

I spoke to my crew leader and we think your house would look much, much better if we were to clear away that pile of wood and garbage behind your garage, take care of that family of raccoons that live there and re-plant a beautiful bush. What do you think?"

And I would say "Thank you, Bob for calling me and proactively thinking of ways to make my house look more beautiful while at the same time exterminating the vermin that live so close to where my dear children play. And even though you overcharged me on that spring cleanup I'm prepared to let bygones be bygones. Bring on the bush!"

Good managers know that if they take care of their existing customers, they'll navigate their way through any type of economy, good or bad. Want to send a stupid, useless marketing brochure? Be my guest, you tree-killing miscreant. Want to get the same results with a lot less money? Pick up the freaking phone.

Judy's Trip To Washington

Judy Simms, a business owner, lives in Texas and went to Washington, D.C. She took her husband, five granddaughters and a large bottle of Jack Daniels.

Judy had a great time. Her granddaughters, aged 6 through 18, had never been to the Capitol. They toured the Washington Monument and the White House. They saw the Lincoln Memorial and Ford's Theatre. It was a pleasant and inspiring experience for everyone. Don't believe me? Judy claims she and her husband only drank half the bottle.

A few weeks after returning from her trip, Judy sent out a marketing piece. She told this story to hundreds of her current and prospective clients. She did this by a mass mailing of oversized postcards. On the front of the postcard was a great picture of everyone in front of the Capitol Building. On the back was a little note that she wrote about the experience, what she learned, how much fun she had, what a great country we live in.

Notice anything missing? No mention of her business. No mention of any products or services that she's selling. Who does this? Who sends a marketing piece that's not trying to sell something? This business owner does. Judy spends thousands of dollars every year on direct-mailing campaigns. She wants to make sure she gets her money's worth. And this is how she does it.

For starters, Judy chose direct mailing as her primary

marketing vehicle. There are many other marketing options at her disposal, such as e-mailing, social networking, telemarketing. But she's a penny pinching business person. Her time and resources are limited. She can't do it all. She needs to choose the right weapon that brings her the best results. So for her, direct mail is the thing. Other people may choose something else. But Judy's got a good approach. And she's sticking to it.

On the bottom of her postcards she has tagline for her company, of course. But she doesn't jam her company's messaging down the reader's throat. Her postcards stand out because they're different this way. And personal. Judy hears from clients, both new and old, how much they enjoy getting them. That's because she's got a good system for sending these pieces.

For one, she makes it personal. She tells stories — like her trip to Washington, or a recent wedding she went to, or a funny night out with her girlfriends. The stories are meant to humanize her and teach the reader a little something about her. They usually emphasize her principles, like her love for family, or her hard work effort, or the importance of being true to your friends. Sometimes she'll sneak in a little correlation to her business. Sometimes not.

Judy's postcards are also unique. She spends on the oversized ones so they really stand out. And she always puts a good graphic on one side too. For her Washington postcard it was a big photo with lots of smiling kids. She sometimes uses free graphics from sites like Morguefile.com. Other times she makes unique pictures and cartoons converted from photos using tools from Befunky.com. Once she converted a photo of herself to a Simpsons' character on Simpsonizeme.com. All of this stands out. It's funny. A little cute, without being sickening. It gets people's attention.

A good entrepreneur, Judy doesn't waste her own valuable time doing this stuff herself. She always outsources the work.

She found a mailing house all the way in Pennsylvania that does a lot of her bulk work. All she does is send them the graphic she's using, a Microsoft Word file of the text and a spreadsheet of names. They take care of the postcard printing and postage and mailing all in one go. She pays about a buck a postcard. A slightly cheaper offering is Printplace.com. They do pretty much the same stuff — just all online. She'll use both services as the mood strikes her. They save her time so she can better use her days talking and working with clients.

Most important, Judy's direct-mail campaigns are consistent. She doesn't buy into any false hopes that she can blast out 5,000 direct-mail pieces and sit back to wait for the phone to ring. She sends her postcards out every quarter. And then she follows many of them up with phone calls and e-mails. Every month she hears from someone who's been receiving her postcards for years, and only now has some work for her. She keeps at it, quarter after quarter. She's patient. She knows that these things don't take overnight.

What does Judy have planned next? A trip to Disney with the girls again. Should be fun. Shame they won't let her bring that bottle of Jack Daniels into the park, though.

Mary Has A Secret

Mary Shaw has a shameful, shameful secret.

No, it has nothing to do with personal hygiene. Or her marriage. Or her kids. She doesn't smoke pot, drink excessively or pop pills. True, she enjoys Sean Hannity's show, which is shameful. But she admits this freely so it's no secret.

Her secret is way more shameful than that. Especially in these technology hyped days.

Mary Shaw owns and operates The Every Day Group – a twenty person health benefits consulting firm. I've been asked not to use her real name or the name of her company because if Mary's shameful secret were to be known by some people she could never show her face in town again.

Are you ready for the secret to be revealed? Well here it is: she sends letters. And faxes. And makes phones calls. To her customers. And to her prospects.

Shocking! Scandalous!

How could she? Has she never heard of this newfangled thing called the internet? Isn't she listening to the media? Doesn't she talk to all those younger folks with greasy hair and black rimmed rectangular glasses who, between puffs on their hookah, lecture us on the new age of electronic communication and social networking tools that are available for business people to launch themselves into the new millennium?

"Whatever," she recently told me. "I still send letters.

And faxes. And make calls."

But Mary's poking fun at us. Her secret isn't as shameful as you think. Sure, she still listens to cassette tapes and reads a newspaper. Sure, she still refers to the rolodex on her desk. She admits that she does a lot of her business the old fashioned way. But she's doing old fashioned things in a new manner. And she's doing these things better than her competition. And contrary to what those younger folks with greasy hair and black rimmed rectangular glasses think about her, she's also using that newfangled thing called the internet. Only she's using it to send letters. And faxes. And make calls. It's fast. It's inexpensive. It's the kind of thing a smart manager does to keep up with her customers and generate more leads.

For faxes, Mary uses two web based faxing services – efax (www.efax.com) and FaxZERO (www.faxzero.com). They're different. eFax lets Mary upload a Word document and then sends it as a fax to her recipient's fax machine. It costs $14 per month which allows 30 pages to be faxed. After that it's $0.10 per page. And faxes can be received too. FaxZERO is a free service where she can send up to two faxes a day (maximum three pages) at no charge, or pay $1.99 for each additional fax (maximum 15 pages).

And calls? Mary uses Voiceshot (www.voiceshot.com) and DialMyCalls (www.dialmycalls.com). These services let her record a message ("Your health insurance benefits are expiring next month – call us!") and then blasts out the message to a pre-defined list of people. Voiceshot charges $0.12 per successful call. DialMyCalls uses a credit system where each credit can be as low as $0.045 per call. But the catch is that you get charged for the call whether it's successful or not. Of course both companies promise to hunt down and kill any customers who misuse their service for telemarketing purposes.

Mary understands something that seems to get lost in today's world of technology hype. Many people don't spend a lot of time reading emails. Many people don't spend a lot of time on Facebook, Twitter or other social media websites. Yet studies have shown that these same people are well-adjusted, friendly and good human beings. Shocking. Shameful. But true.

So Mary wants to make sure that these well-adjusted, friendly and good human beings, who are also customers and prospective customers, hear from her. She understands that people get their information from all sorts of different places. Some actually read their mail. Others still (gasp!) have a fax machine. And, omigod, there are some walking the earth who actually get phone calls instead of sending text messages. Wow. No one under the age of 25 would believe that one. But it's true. It's true!

Shameful isn't it? Mary sending letters and faxes and making phone calls. It's a terrible secret she keeps. Let's hope we never find out who the "real" Mary is. And let's hope that we all learn a few things from this smart business person.

Hello? Still There?

A few summers ago my family took an RV trip to Niagara Falls, N.Y. We had a blast. On the way we visited Cooperstown, where we stood in line for two hours to look at Babe Ruth's jockstrap. We paid $40 per night for an asphalt parking space in an RV park with a view of the local diner. I left dents in a few parked cars in an upstate New York Walmart (YOU try and steer a 30-foot truck around those corners). We even spoke to Canadians, but not too much, thank goodness.

All in all, the trip was a success. The RV was fine. The place where we rented it from (I'll call them "RV-A-Go-Go") provided a great service, even answering our panicked calls one Friday night when our toilet decided to work in reverse. But something kind of bothered me afterwards. It was after we limped back to RV-A-Go-Go and turned in the keys.

We never heard from them again. Not a phone call. Nothing in the mail or e-mail. Not a peep.

I don't get this. Is the RV business so profitable? Is there such an endless backlog of short, bald, sunburnt dads like me who take their kids on RV trips that a business like RV-A-Go-Go doesn't feel the need to do any marketing?

Good managers do whatever they can to keep their customers coming back. They use inexpensive tools to keep in touch. They know that finding new customers costs significantly more than selling additional products and services to their existing customers.

One way they do this is through e-mail. Why was I not at least invited to receive an e-mail newsletter from RV-A-Go-Go? I wouldn't mind getting an RV or camping tip sent to me every month. I'd be interested in any special deals or offers they might have for a weekend or holiday getaway. I might even consider taking my family back to Canada again.

RV-A-Go-Go could use an e-mail marketing service like Constant Contact (www.constantcontact.com). A ton of other smart business owners have already found this service — it's ranked among the top 500 websites in the world.

There are other good e-mail marketing services (Feelbreeze.com, Jangomail.com and Campaigner.com). These services are inexpensive, easy to use and safe.

Besides offering a free trial, they generally cost about $50-100 per month to send up to 10,000 e-mails. I doubt even the crack marketing team at RV-A-Go-Go is handling that many customers. There's also a bunch of ready made templates too. That means that you don't need that greasy 17-year-old Web designer who's going to charge you $200 per hour just to design a slick e-mail.

E-mail marketing services like the ones I mentioned monitor their customers for potential spammers. When you blast out an e-mail, you'll find that most of the major Internet service providers will let your messages pass because they're originating from firms that do a little due diligence and have known services ... not some unknown computer traceable somewhere in the Philippines (or perhaps ... Canada?).

The services also manage people who opt-out of your mailing and give reports to show who actually opened or read your messages. You can keep your customer list with them or upload it from a spreadsheet every month. It's pretty easy.

I get a lot of spam. I don't read those messages about print cartridges, stock tips or Viagra (well, maybe some of the Viagra ones). But a monthly newsletter of RV or camping tips would be pretty cool. I could be enticed to do another little trip.

Don't be like RV-A-Go-Go. Don't let good customers forget about you. You can keep an inexpensive relationship going by using e-mail marketing tools. And do visit Niagara Falls. But try not to feed any Canadians while you're there.

The Secret of Smart E-Mail Marketing

Small-business owners have monkeyed around with mass e-mail campaigns for years. We started out with software like Outlook, ACT!, and GoldMine, which merged and lobbed generic messages to groups of customers and prospects. But there's more to e-mail marketing than just blasting out messages.

More recently, many of us have turned to e-mail marketing vendors to hone our electronic attacks. These services manage campaigns by allowing recipients to opt out and feeding the interested with more information. Better yet, these easy-to-use, database-driven tools--many customizable, down to the logos and graphics--are also cheap: usually under $100 per month to blast thousands of e-mails.

But just because e-mail campaigns are becoming more common doesn't mean their architects are getting better at crafting them. The big problem: relevance--as in, the lack of it.

This isn't rocket science. When Staples sends a message plugging free shipping, that's a lot less compelling than a special offer on printer cartridges you've purchased before. Likewise, learning that Borders is offering 30% off best-sellers is nice, but how about 30% off titles by your favorite author or on a subject you're interested in?

Of course, the fact that you can operate a car doesn't mean you can drive it very well (just ask Britney Spears). The same goes for e-mail campaigns: Blasting a product ad to millions isn't particularly effective--unless you're hawking mortgages, stock tips or Viagra.

"The more relevant the message to the recipients' interests, the more likely it will rise above the other messages," says Eric S. Groves, formerly a senior vice president at Constant Contact. Remember them from my last chapter?

Groves should know. Constant Contact provides e-mail marketing services to over 150,000 small companies. It also offers free guidance, including live Webinars, recorded tutorials, white papers and a newsletter called "Hints & Tips." As for performance, Constant Contact manages to successfully deliver 97 out of every 100 e-mails, according to Return Path, an independent e-mail tracking firm.

It's not that sending the right message to the appropriate people is hard--it's that too few business owners take the time to do it.

Mark Sperling is one of them. His company, Girls Learn To Ride, teaches women extreme sports, like skateboarding, BMX, motocross and other activities most of us would avoid. Sperling knows his customers have a variety of interests: A snowboarder might not be thrilled to know about the best waves on the West Coast, and a teenager couldn't care less about spa treatments for older athletes.

That's why Sperling takes the time to carve up his audience before trying to reach them. "We have segmented lists," he says. "That way, we can send out relevant e-mails about upcoming events in a sport that matches the profile of the athlete." The same logic applies to different product lines.

Sperling sends out six to eight messages a month. These include a newsletter, which goes to his entire database; a weekly news e-mail for those who ask to receive it; "event update" or custom e-mails segmented by age, location or sports interest; and periodic surveys. Costs: about $150 a month to Constant Contact. Sperling also pays a few bucks to cover the time his in-house staff spends tailoring the messages. Result: Click-through rates have jumped 10% to 35%.

For all that smart targeting, it's still hard to get people to open e-mails unless they recognize the sender immediately. According to a survey from DoubleClick, 60% of respondents cite the "From" line as the most important factor motivating them to open e-mails.

If a brand name is more memorable than a personal name, use it in the "From" line. Avoid using generic addresses like sales@ or info@. Also, keep the "From" name consistent and recognizable in all of your e-mails.

The "From" line is important, but the subject line is where you set the trap. The key is attracting attention with imagery and specificity. Example: A subject line that reads "Five Plants Deer Won't Eat" is more compelling than "Monthly Newsletter."

Remember: When it comes to e-mail marketing, it's all about quality, not quantity. Take the time to do it right.

Creating a Service Community

Everyone knows that online social networks like FaceBook and LinkedIn are powerful marketing tools. Throw in Twitter (which lets you blast out ultra-brief electronic diary entries called "tweets"), easy-to-create blogs and online forums, and business people have a fat cache of weapons for attacking just about any kind of customer.

But social networks are about more than just getting the good word out. For the most innovative businesses, they're about providing extraordinary customer service.

"There's a fundamental flaw in the way people approach social community websites," says Mike McDerment, chief executive of FreshBooks, a Toronto-based online-invoicing outfit that mainly serves small companies. "They think that FaceBook or LinkedIn is some kind of marketing thing. For most people, it's a wrong assumption."

To ensure that he offers the best, up-to-the minute support, McDerment uses a multipronged online attack. While it's hard to measure the actual return on investment on these initiatives, taken together the benefits are twofold, he says. First, the Web tools allow him to save money and time by spreading customer-support duties among all 30 employees. Second, they enable him to corral valuable feedback from customers.

McDerment's online strategy starts with his website, which features a custom-made forum that runs on free, open-source software called PunBB. Here, readers can post questions, and FreshBooks (and other) users can respond. Customers can search the answers by type of question, post their own responses or just make general comments.

The site also has links to other online guides on related topics. The forums generate a new post about every 15 minutes throughout the business day; the company aims to respond to everything in real time, but certainly within an hour.

McDerment also fired up a blog--called "Fresh Thinking"--to keep customers even more up to date, on everything from new products and services to his own thoughts on the online billing industry at large. While the forum is focused on fielding questions about FreshBooks' service, the blog aims to share Freshbooks' perspective on running a growing small business--everything from collecting money to managing a sales staff.

"Our blog posts are not all about FreshBooks," says McDerment. "They have a broader appeal to the small-business community as a whole."

How about FaceBook, LinkedIn and Twitter? FreshBooks has real estate in each online community, via "friends" or connections. Here, too, the company responds to users' questions and comments. It also posts updates about new products, as well as photos and videos of people using FreshBooks in action, enhancing the connection with potential customers.

The beauty of McDerment's multifaceted attack is how fast and often he can stay in touch with customers. Those who go to Freshbooks' Facebook page or to its blog can sign up for RSS feeds, e-mail updates or text messages about, say, when a new version of the software is released or when an annoying bug has been fixed.

Another benefit: feedback. McDerment gets an unvarnished view of how his company is performing. Take, for instance, its report card service, which allows customers to benchmark against other companies, using a percentile ranking.

"Turns out the way we implemented the percentile reporting--which counted on different colors to communicate different percentiles--didn't work for color-blind users," says McDerment. "So we changed the design to a [percentile] bar rather than using a color."

Not that this stuff is so easy. Responding to forums, administering a blog and interacting with customers takes time---a precious commodity for most companies. To compensate, McDerment gets as many employees involved as possible. The challenge: making sure everyone is speaking with one voice. That's why everyone at FreshBooks, including the executive team, spends the first three months in customer service and support.

"We want our entire team to learn our product, our customer and our culture," says McDerment. "Everyone spends a significant period of time learning the right answers and the correct way to communicate them."

Yes, social networks are a great marketing tool, but that's selling customers short. When it comes to providing great service, "we go to the community," says McDerment. "We don't ask them to come to us."

Beware Social Media Marketing Myths

Comedian Jim Gaffigan has a suggestion for preparing a Hot Pockets frozen entrée: "Take out of package. Place directly in toilet." Gaffigan is not a big fan of Hot Pockets. He doesn't like exercise, either. But he loves bacon. "Without bacon, no one would even know what a water chestnut is," he says. Gaffigan's also a fan of social networking sites.

You'll see him on Facebook, Twitter, and even MySpace. He keeps fans up to date on his concerts, albums, TV appearances—and naps. In short, he's a social networking success story. For a one-man band like Gaffigan, who probably has a decent amount of free time between eating bacon and being on stage, social networks and blogs have proved effective vehicles for marketing his business and staying close to his audience. But for many business owners, social networking is as valuable as a Hot Pocket is nutritious.

We've been misled as to the benefits of social networking sites. Many of us are finding that these tools do not live up to the hype, especially for small business. Once we start digging deeper, we're finding a lot of challenges. Are you thinking of using Facebook, Twitter, or the like in your business? Before you go any further, consider the following myths:

1. Social media sites are free.

Using social media sites isn't as easy or cheap as many people think. Sure, most let you set up an account for free. And you can integrate other services, such as your blog or Google's

YouTube videos, at no charge. But there's a significant cost: your time. Because there's nothing worse than a site that's not current. And to keep it current, someone's going to need to spend time. This includes responding to visitors' questions, posting brilliant thoughts, adding graphics, and monitoring activity—basically trying to generate buzz.

Comedian Gaffigan seems to peruse his sites all the time. Bacon is still yummy days after it's cooked. But old information—a stagnant site, comments left without response—are death in the social networking community. I recently moderated a small business town hall forum. The company sponsoring the event had two full-time "social media writers" covering the event. They recognize that keeping a presence on these sites takes resources. Unfortunately, many of us don't have that kind of time—or cash—on hand.

2. Social media sites are a great place to find new customers.

In fact, the major sites aren't necessarily the best places for a business owner. Some of the most avid users of Facebook are pimply adolescents and goth teenagers. Sure, there's a growing number of fortysomethings—but many are merely nostalgic to check out boyfriends and girlfriends from their youth to see how fat and bald they've become. Whatever they're doing on Facebook, it's typically not engaging with a small business brand. Twitter has millions of users, but apparently only four of them actually understand what it does and spend much time updating their tweets. Are these the people who will buy the plastic polymer gaskets your company manufacturers? I don't think so.

Where, then, should a business person go online? Often the best social networking sites are specific to their needs. For example, Intuit's customers have their own small business community. Another good one is Bank of America's small business community. You can Google them. I'll also talk more about these sites in later chapters. These and others like them are tailored for people who run their own companies. Industry groups have started their own communities. Technology manufacturers have them, too. They used to be called "newsgroups" and "support sites," but now the vernacular is "communities." Same thing. These are places where business people go to post and answer questions about product problems, customer service queries, saving money on taxes, generating leads, hiring employees, eating bacon. You don't hear about these sites much because they're boring as hell. Then again, so are most of us who manage companies.

3. You need to be on all the big sites.

Besides spending a lot of time and effort, business people I know who have succeeded with social networking sites generally focus on just a few of them. Although he dabbles in Twitter, Gaffigan's main vehicle is Facebook. Some companies prefer to build a business community on LinkedIn. I know a few nerdy guys who live on a couple of technology community sites and generate leads from them by consistently responding to questions and helping other users. Just because the media says it's cool to tweet doesn't mean it has anything to do with your business. If you're going to to frequent social community sites, don't spread yourself too thin. Most of the guys I know who use these things successfully pick their weapon and give it their all.

4. Social networking sites are for marketing.

Baloney. I've learned from other smart business owners that social communities are not for marketing. They're for service. In the last chapter I spoke to FreshBooks CEO Mike McDerment, who views these places as ways to get closer to his customers and respond to their needs. "Wherever they are, that's where I'll go," he told me. By providing quick and helpful customer service through these sites, he believes he will foster loyalty and satisfaction, resulting in more sales. In his own way, Gaffigan does the same. Makes sense. So whenever someone tells you that you should explore social networking "marketing," you should run in the other direction. It's the service, stupid.

5. Social networking is the future.

Really? Some of these cool and trendy sites aren't going to be so cool and trendy in the near future. The percentage of Twitter users in a given month who return the following month has languished below 30% for most of the past year, according to Nielsen Wire. And MySpace has been suffering a serious decline in monthly visitor traffic. Remember GeoCities? Yahoo! shut it down. A lot of business people aren't thrilled about committing time and resources to a vanishing trend. Maybe social networking is a permanent phenomenon. That doesn't mean its main players today will be the main players tomorrow.

So should a business person use social media sites for his company? Maybe. Then again, maybe other customer service approaches make more sense. Remember newsletters, phone calls and support, seminars, partnering, and the like? Just because the media have determined that social networking is "in" doesn't mean your customers are there. Hot Pockets may be a tasty late night snack, but you may want to think how you'll feel the next morning!

We Don't Need No Stinkin' Websites

A few months ago I was at a technology conference and things were abuzz. The results of a recent survey had just been announced and—gasp—it found that an astonishing 40% of small businesses don't have a website (another survey put the number closer to 60%). How could this be? Considering there are more than 20 million small businesses in the U.S., are we actually saying that something like 10 million small businesses in this country don't have a website? Shocking. Ignorant. Appalling.

"Oh, they just soooo don't get it," said one conference attendee, a turtleneck-and-vest-wearing, greasy-haired propeller head drinking a Red Bull. Others around him clucked their agreement while sending this shocking news to their Twitter accounts by way of their Apple iPhones.

Are those small business owners as naive as these very smart and witty technologists believe? I don't think so. Most are probably smarter than many who attended the conference. Why? Because millions of business owners may know something that we're not prepared to admit. Some people don't really need a website at all. Maybe a web page. But not a website.

First, let me explain the difference. A web page is simple. A web page has basic, but important, information—like contact data and maybe a photo or two. A web page doesn't need a lot of maintenance. It doesn't need a lot of creativity.

And it certainly doesn't need any turtleneck-and-vest-wearing, greasy-haired propeller heads drinking Red Bull to maintain it. In fact, it can be hosted for less than $10 a month by any one of a hundred companies that do that sort of thing. Some companies, like Synthasite and Weebly let you set up, for free, very simple websites that are akin to pages. Other popular destinations, like Facebook or LinkedIn, can also be used.

A site is, by definition, a collection of many web pages. I'm sure you've seen them. Lots of pretty pictures. Flash videos. Pop-up windows. High-definition graphics. And those are just the NSFW sites I visit. I hear business sites have a lot of this stuff, too.

But here's a fun exercise for you to do. Go to Amazon. com's Alexa and download its free toolbar. Whenever you go to a website, Alexa will show you where that site ranks in its universe of websites. Alexa.com has its limitations. But for a free site, it provides some pretty interesting information. For example, you know the guy who spent a ton of money with one of those turtleneck-and-vest-wearing, greasy-haired propeller heads to plan, create, develop, implement, and then maintain a website for his hardware store? Well, his site is ranked No. 98,388,756,442. This is just a few spots behind my company's website. Which means that no one, other than his mother (and my mother), is visiting it.

Want to get it listed higher? Then go ahead and pay one of the search engine optimization vampires a pint of blood so you can catch a glimpse of it somewhere on the first few pages of Google. Wow. More money spent so people can find out your address and phone number.

So what's the point?

Websites cost money—not just to host, but to create. If you're going to have a website for your business, you're probably going to want it to look really cool, hip, and professional. Like the Drudge Report. You'll need to take time to develop it. You may need to pay a consultant. One of those turtleneck-and-vest-wearing, greasy-haired propeller heads. And for Pete's sake you're going to need to keep it up to date. Your products may be obsolete and your services have never adapted to the times. But that doesn't mean your website has to get stale.

But is this really necessary? Can all those site-less small business owners be wrong? They're not trying to shock. They're not trying to grab attention. They're just trying to save some money. Marketing dollars are limited. For many, sinking a bunch of dollars into a website may not be the best return on investment.

Oh sure, if you're in the Internet porn business, or sell things online, then this is an entirely different story. Or if you're looking to replace all of your marketing materials and send prospects and customers online to learn in detail about your products and services, then it makes sense to a have a full-fledged site. Or if you're going to use your site to provide customer service, manuals, videos, and a knowledge base, you'll want a vehicle to do this.

But gee, many of the business people I know—those incredible, pathetic, dismal, wretched losers who so shock the turtleneck-and-vest-wearing, greasy-haired crowd—don't necessarily have those needs. They are gas station owners, restauranteurs, insurance agents, shopkeepers. They're CPAs, architects, landscapers, plumbers, and electricians. They're not selling books online or running auctions. They're not distributing software or hosting phone services. They're not complex. They're investing elsewhere. They're OK with no website.

When was the last time I visited the site for the corner Exxon guy or the sub shop across from my office? To see the price of gas? To get nutrition info on a ham on rye sandwich?

If you search the Web, you'll find lots of people writing about how small business owners must have a website. Dig a little further and guess what? Many of the people shouting how absolutely critical it is for a small business to have a website are—drum roll, please—in the business of helping small businesses create websites. Surprise! Despite what all the business experts—including the turtleneck-and-vest-wearing classes—may say, websites are not an absolute necessity.

Good business people invest wisely and for the most return. They're not in business to run a site just because it's cool or hip. Many people I know are fine with a simple and professional web page. Let the turtleneck-and-vest-wearing, greasy-haired geeks suck their fees from someone else.

Charge For Shipping...And Handling

Are you sitting down? Because I've got shocking news for you. That automatic banana polisher that you bought at 3AM on channel 388 really didn't cost $19.95. It's $19.95 plus $5.00 shipping AND handling.

What does "...and handling" mean? Is this something that was invented by those people who sell banana polishers, Ginza knives and other essentials on late night TV? And how come whenever you buy one of those electric cat painting tools from one of those commercials the shipping "and handling" charges are a flat amount, like $15.00 or $25.00? Is it really that perfectly exact?

Not exactly. But the national marketers have figured it out. They've got it down to a science. They ship millions of robo-vacuums, laser-guided toenail clippers and organic hair-growing kits every year. They don't want to waste time calculating shipping costs. And they certainly don't want to pay for shipping costs either.

These guys are always looking to shake a few more pennies out of the sale. That's because producing a gumball cleaning device for $1.00 and selling it for $19.95 is just not profitable enough. So what do they do? They round up the shipping and they charge for "handling" too...all in a nice flat fee.

What a bunch of ruthless, cold-hearted, callous jerks! Now that we got that out of the way....how can we be just like them?

As a public service, I thought I'd walk you through how you can calculate the "Handling" costs in your business.

First, take the annual cost for people working in shipping and add it to the annual cost for people working in your office. Then add to that the annual cost of supplies and postage needed, plus the annual cost of your golf club membership. And don't forget the annual cost of that vacation home in Florida. Now you've got your Total Handling Cost. Next, divide this amount by the number of products shipped each year to reach your Cost Per Product Shipped. Finally, plug this amount with whatever number necessary so you can arrive at $25.00. And there you have it: your "handling charge".

No customer is going to ask you for an actual calculation of this cost, especially if it's in the range of what they're used to paying elsewhere. Some customers may balk. If this becomes a sticking point then you can be gracious to them. You can show them your good faith and "how much you value their relationship" by reducing or waiving the fee.

But most customers, like you, will shrug and accept the charge. That could be an extra $25 you're earning per shipment. That may not sound like a lot, but if you do just 10 shipments a week, guess what? It's an extra $13,000 per year!

Now that you're clued-in about these handling charges, why are you still paying them? The next time you get this billed by a vendor, jump up and down. Scream. Complain. Threaten to take your business elsewhere. Do all the things that your customers do to you! Be a penny pincher. Many, if not most, of your vendors will cave and reduce or waive the charge. That results in even more savings for you. Now you can take that $25.00 and buy another banana polisher!

Profiting from the MLB

Duffy's Irish Pub in Washington DC had a promotion. Every time Washington Nationals (and former Phillies) outfield Jayson Werth homered anyone in the bar at that time watching the game (and wearing Nats gear) will get a free shot. I love this. I love this not that I'm a Nationals fan (I'm not. I'm a Phillies fan). Not that I'm a Jayson Werth fan (I am...c'mon Phillies fans, the guy will forever be in our hearts as an instrumental part of that 2008 world championship team).

I love it as a business owner who appreciates other business owners that come up with innovative ways to market their businesses. Why not leverage off the Nationals? They're likely to do pretty well this year and their fan base is growing. Why not take a sliver of the team's publicity and turn it into some more business for your business?

Tying your marketing to your local baseball team can bring in those fans that were never your customers before. If it's innovative you may get some free press out of it, like Duffy's. It makes things more interesting for your employees. And frankly it just makes your boring work day a little more fun.

So how to profit from your hometown team this summer? Consider these ten brilliant ideas.

1. Targeted promos. As a kid I remember that whenever

a Phillies player hit a home run it meant a box of TastyKakes for some lucky fan. I remember the local Daily News ran a home run payoff contest awarding money whenever a homer was hit and lots of money for a grand slam (do they still do this? I think they do). During the course of the baseball season, pick a target and promote it. Duffy's gives shots whenever Werth hits a home run. How about a free item every time your home team wins a game? Or a 10% discount whenever there's a shutout? If you're bored, change the target every month. If your team starts losing, make it all about losing more. Mets fans: pay close attention to that last piece of advice.

2. Take your best people to games. Why do the big law and accounting firms buy up those tickets to sporting events? Because they're rich of course! And they're also smart. Small businesses can do the same. And we don't have to be ruthless bastards either. Buy a full or partial season ticket plan. If it's too late, scoop up tickets on Craigslist or Ebay. It will cost you a few thousand bucks. But man up! The returns can be significant. Use these tickets and take your best customers, partners, vendors and...yes...employees to games. Try not to just give these tickets away, even if you're from Pittsburgh. I agree it could be painful to watch the Pirates on the field, but avert your eyes and focus on your companion. Unlike most other professional sports, baseball is so boring there's nothing better to do than to sit around and talk business. And you might just get more business out of the evening.

3. Give stuff away. If you don't want to do targeted promos then just buy a bunch of cheap gear related to your hometown team and give it away on certain days. If you're a Phillies fan then it could be something fitting like "Saturday is Phillies baseball cap day." Or if you're a Mets fan then try: "Monday is Mets sanitary napkin day." Something like that. Promotional gear is sold everywhere and can be inexpensive. There's no legal issue if you're just giving it away. But it

41

demonstrates your pride (or your insanity) about your local team and builds up a little community support.

4. Run a baseball-theme contest. Have your customers fill out a form (online and with their permission-based email addresses....remember you're building up your VIP list for future marketing) where they can guess how many home runs a certain player will hit this month. Or how many beers the Red Sox will drink by the 7th inning. Or how many days until Ozzie Guillen gets chased out of Miami. Let your customers choose their own all star team. Even if your team falls out of the running you can still have fun with baseball related contests.

5. Get involved with a charity. Instead of being so selfish, why not think of others for a change? Pick a charity and run baseball themed promotions to raise money. Something like "for every Cardinals win, we'll donate $100 bucks to XYZ charity (which is not supported by Albert Pujols)." Spread the guilt and invite your customers and partners to match your generous donation. Don't worry – you'll still get the marketing and public relations credit and you'll come off as a super sensitive person too. Just make sure you get to present one of those giant cardboard checks to the charity at their next luncheon and have someone call the local newspapers beforehand.

6. Do a community thing with your team. All the MLB teams do community service stuff. The Phillies, for example, have a new "Phillies Phitness" program (spelling is not our strength in Philly). They also award standout teachers and students. They run local baseball events and educational programs. They do the environmental thing. And if you look at your team's website under "community" you'll find a schedule of all their pending community–related events. Even the L.A. Dodgers give something back to their community, which is the kind of behavior you don't see very often in L.A. So get involved. Be a sponsor. Give your employees time off to participate. And then promote the community organization as part of your company's marketing.

7. Make your baseball passion part of your company's communications. Newsletters are boring. Technical specifications are boring. Marketing emails are boring. So spice them up with something completely different: your love of baseball, your love of your local team. Maybe include in each newsletter a little insightful commentary about your team's prospects. Or a completely unrelated piece of baseball trivia in your next marketing piece. It changes things up a bit. It shows your human side. It creates interest. It may grab the attention of a baseball loving prospect or customer. It shows hometown pride. Including a baseball item in what would otherwise be another boring piece of corporate communications creates a fun discussion angle that may help you get to know your customers better.

8. Create a baseball rivalry. Choose a friendly competitor in another town and create a rivalry. Mayors do this every year in the post season. Put your money where your mouth is. Every time your team plays your rival you wager something particularly local to give away to your enemy: a cheese-steak if you're from Philly, a cowboy hat if you're from Houston, a bag of marijuana if you're from San Francisco. Get your customers involved. Take this rivalry with you to the next industry trade show. It'll create some attention and be a fun thing for others to talk about. If the rivalry makes it to the post season (no, not you Mets fans) then turn into a story for the local media. They'll love it.

9. Create new baseball partnerships. Find a business locally that has nothing to do with your own and create a baseball partnership. Together agree to give away free stuff to each other's customers if your local team accomplishes something. Maybe give away free sushi from the local Japanese restaurant every time Yu Darvish wins a game. Or a bottle of vitamins from a nearby health food store whenever Manny Ramirez hits a home run. Your customers benefit. Your partners get exposure to your customer base. You can probably even get the odd tuna roll for free once in a while too.

10. Advertise. This is the most expensive proposition of all. But there's justification here. Most teams have their major corporate sponsors of course. But there are plenty of opportunities to purchase ads on websites, programs and other materials offered out by the club. 45,000 fans attending and millions watching each game is nothing to sneeze at. Oops... sorry, I got those numbers from the Real Madrid soccer website. The average numbers for the MLB are much lower than that. But they're still pretty good and worth considering in your marketing plans.

Profit with your team. Have fun. And good luck to everyone next season. Except for the Mets, of course.

Ways to Increase Revenues

Today and in the Future

Sales Tips from Paris Hilton

As business owners, we should all be more like Paris Hilton.

Of course, I don't mean filming ourselves having sex with our partners and distributing the video over the Internet (my video would more likely end up on Comedy Central rather than a porn site). And I don't mean staying out all night at wild parties, doing drugs, binge drinking and lying around all day accomplishing nothing. Most of us already did this in college.

I'm talking about negotiating ... Paris Hilton-style.

Now, don't discount what she's accomplished. Remember when she was in jail a few years ago? And then out? And then back in? All of that crying, whining and complaining not only brought her even more public attention, but also bought her a few extra days at her home (instead of a jail cell) and then in a cushy medical ward. And those few extra pampered days, when compared to the actual days she ultimately served, turns into a pretty nifty little discount on time served, I'm sure you'll agree.

A whiny, vapid, brain-dead, spoiled little brat? Au contraire! Paris Hilton used some very savvy techniques to negotiate her jail time discount. Let's take a closer look at her best tactics so that we can learn from the master at work.

"But officer, I didn't know my license was suspended!" Playing dumb during a negotiation is always a good ploy. Paris is a natural at this. We are humbled by her skills. A good

negotiator should always act surprised and plenty ignorant when pricing is given. Conveniently forgetting key facts is a good weapon, too. You might get a break this way.

"I won't have any privacy!" Paris was afraid a photo of her on a jail cell toilet would make its way around the Internet. She's afraid of public embarrassment. You can do the same. You can tell a salesperson that you're concerned about being embarrassed in front of your colleagues and therefore will be checking prices that others paid. Knowing that you're doing a little comparative shopping, the seller will be less likely to gouge you.

"It's unfair! Mommy!" Paris' agonized courtroom cries as she was led off to serve her time (in that isolated and comfortable medical ward) really touched my heart, as I'm sure it did with other concerned citizens across the country. Sometimes you can take advantage of a salesperson who feels sorry for you too. Like Paris, an accomplished negotiator should also cry out "Injustice!" when discussing price. Turn on the tears. Stamp your feet. At the very least an unsympathetic salesperson may cut the price just to avoid any further tantrums.

"My daddy's going to be angry with you!" Maybe that sheriff who let Paris out early was a little intimidated by the power of the Hilton family. Paris certainly did her homework. How else could she have known that the good cop/bad cop ploy is so effective? Don't ignore this great method either. Make sure to let the salesperson know that there's a behind-the-scenes "daddy" too -- maybe it's a partner, or your spouse, or someone else who you have to answer to before making the purchase.

"If you let me out you can party with me and Nicky." A night out with Paris and Nicky? Giggity! Paris sure knows the power of bartering. What favors do you have to barter or offer a salesperson to negotiate a lower price? Maybe you'll commit to a longer service plan? Or you can refer him to some of your customers or friends?

See what I mean? Paris can teach us a few things, too. Let's use her terrible ordeal as a lesson. Let us all benefit from the overwhelming challenges that she has faced. We should not let Paris' bravery go in vain. Let us be inspired by her courage and tenacity. In future negotiations let us cry, whine, complain and have tantrums. We might just save a few bucks in the process. At the very least it could keep us out of jail.

Hey, Big Tom... Disco's Dead

Attention, sales people. Jane, small business owner, wants you to know something: It's 2013. Not 1978.

Not that 1978 was so bad. Jane was still in high school. Her favorite movie was "Grease" and her favorite song was "Three Times A Lady" by the Commodores. Hmmm. Come to think of it, maybe 1978 was pretty bad after all.

A thousand miles west, Big Tom (yes, that's what they called him) was just graduating college and starting a job selling insurance. He read books written by those famous sales gurus. Here's where he learned how to "close the sale." There was the "one-call close" and the "two-call close." There were all these little deceptive ways into tricking your prospect to "sign the contract." There were all these tactics for "getting the appointment" and "overcoming objections." Big Tom was learning from the best. The best that 1978 had to offer.

Fast forward 35 years. Jane now runs a successful architectural firm. True, she still sings along to the songs from "Grease" when they play on the radio. But thankfully, she's moved on from the Lionel Ritchie thing. Unfortunately, Big Tom is still stuck in a time warp.

Big Tom now sells phone systems. Not an easy job, especially in these tough times. But that wasn't going to get Tom down. Especially when Jane responded to a cold call he made and told him that she might be interested in purchasing a phone system for her company. Can you hear Big Tom salivating on the other end of the line? He was ready to sell, sell, sell!

Big Tom was all about "selling the appointment." "Let's meet," he begged Jane. "I need to assess your company's needs." Reluctantly, Jane agreed to get together for a "quick meeting." That was a mistake.

Big Tom, dressed in a three-piece suit and a flowery tie, looked like something out of a sales training video. Poor Jane. Her "quick" meeting turned into a three-hour event. Tom insisted on walking her through brochure after brochure. He brought with him equipment to demo. He guided her, line by line, through the maintenance agreements and other paperwork. All she wanted was some information to do some research. But Big Tom, still playing by those old sales rules, had intentions to close the sale right there!

Jane managed to fend off Big Tom that day, but apparently the battle had just begun.

For weeks afterwards Tom called and e-mailed her. At first he was just "checking in" and "following up." But then the calls got more aggressive. Big Tom started setting up appointments that she didn't agree to "just to get together and go over things." He would send her quote after quote offering incentives that had expiration dates that were "coming up shortly." He pushed and pushed. Because that's what the Sales Gurus told him to do.

After a month of this, Jane had had enough. She stopped responding to Big Tom altogether.

Big Tom's a nice guy. He sells decent products. And his prices weren't so bad either. There's no reason why a buyer like Jane shouldn't buy from him. And maybe she will. But what Big Tom doesn't realize is that his schedule is not Jane's schedule. She doesn't need to help him make his quarterly sales quota. She has other priorities and other things to spend her money on right now. Sure, she'd like to get a new phone system at some point, but she'll be ready to buy when she's ready to buy. It's her decision. Not Big Tom's.

But not according to those sales gurus. They tell sales guys like Big Tom to try things like The Choice Close (Mr. Prospect, would you prefer to buy A or B?) or the Ben Franklin Close (show them how a penny saved is like a penny earned) or the most arrogant one of all: the Assumption Close (that's where you just write up the order and hand it to the prospect, as if it's all part of the plan).

As business people, we don't like to be forced into anything. In fact, the reason why we're running our own businesses instead of working for someone is that we like to be as much in control of things as we can. The last thing we need is for some sales guy, even a nice sales guy like Big Tom, to be pushing us into appointments, contracts and sales when we're not ready to do anything.

Big Tom has to stop reading those old sales books and enter into the 21st century. Nowadays, it's all about low-key selling. Jane wants to be educated. She wants information. She wants to be able to do her own research. She wants to build a relationship with a sales guy on her terms. She wants to think about the deal and discuss with others. She wants to look up reviews on the Internet. She wants to visit a company's website on her own, when she likes. She wants jewelry (well, don't all women want jewelry?).

In other words, she wants to be left alone. That doesn't mean that she wants Big Tom to ignore her. It's just that when she needs him, she'll contact him. She's OK with him checking in briefly once in a while or sending her stuff by e-mail or mail if it'll help her in the process. But she doesn't want to be sold. She'll decide when she's buying.

So how's Jane's new phone system? Well, she's still mulling it over. There are other options she's considering (that's a whole other story). But if Big Tom plays his cards the right way, and if she does decide to go for a phone system,

51

he'll be first on her list to call. That's how to sell to a business owner like Jane in the 21st century.

What the Airlines Teach Us

A bunch of airlines announced a few years ago that they're now going to start charging all passengers for things like checked bags and blankets. This is in addition to charging extra for food, drinks, movies and lap dancers. OK, just kidding about the lap dancers. That's in first class only.

The point is that everyone was up in arms about these extra charges. But is this really such a big deal? I'm not a fan of the airline industry either. I don't like paying more for a flight to Pittsburgh than to London during the week. I still can't believe how all systems suddenly fail the minute there's an unexpected delay. Being less than five-and-a-half feet tall, I still can't understand how normal-size adults squeeze themselves into today's airline seats.

But charging for services like baggage handling and drinks? This is not new. It's called unbundling. Floormats and radios used to be included in a new car's price. Now you're buying them extra. HBO used to be included with your cable package. Now you're paying extra for it. A baked potato used to come with your steak. Now for your $50 you get ... a steak. The other day I had to buy ... BUY ... an extra little container of salad dressing for my takeout meal. Everything's a la carte.

Big companies are nickel and diming us left and right. And most of us, as customers, grumble and accept it.

My cable company charges me a $4.98 monthly "franchise line fee." My payroll company charges me a $10 "delivery fee." Ever check out your phone bill? My company gets charged for a monthly "federal universal service fee" (67 cents) and a "federal subscriber line charge fee" ($5.94). They pass through a state "relay surcharge" (8 cents), "federal excise tax" (27 cents) and a "gross receipts tax surcharge" (35 cents).

I'm not done yet! Our utility company charged us $1.67 last month for "balancing service charges," $3.58 for "gas cost adjustment charges" and $11.05 for "distribution charges."

What the heck are all these charges? Of course, if you ask these companies there's going to be a rational explanation for each one. There always is. I'm sure they're completely legal and justified. No more or less than charging for checked bags or soft drinks on a plane.

But do you notice that no matter how big a company is ... there's no charge too small? My phone company may make a billion dollars a year, but that's not going to stop it from passing through an 8 cent relay charge. And why not?

As business managers we can learn from this. What legitimate expenses are we incurring that are not being charged through to our customers?

What about freight charges? Are they all being billed back? How about special charges for expediting orders? Why not overtime charges when a client demands it. Are you billing back all out of pocket expenses? Parking? Tolls? Meals? Do you have a case for including an administrative, copying or delivery charge on your invoice? Law firms find a way to do this.

Think about how much overtime you paid your people last year. Or how many packages you sent overnight courier because your customer demanded something the next day. Were all these extra expenses, incurred on our customers' behalf, billed back to them? We're business people, for goodness sakes, not philanthropists.

Do we seem miserly going back to our customers for a $2 parking reimbursement? No more miserly than the phone company collecting that 8 cent relay charge. Why don't we do the same?

Good managers try every means possible, within reason and keeping an eye on the competition, to pass through their costs. The phone company knows this. The airlines know this. Your utility company knows this. They'll squeeze every 8 pennies out of their customers that they can, rather than sucking it up themselves. This is business in the 21st century. Maybe we should stop being so outraged and start applying these practices.

What We Teach the Airlines

Did anyone ever see that Oprah show where she discussed the sex lives of Catholic nuns? Apparently some of the sisters compared their sexual urges to that of "chocolate cravings".

OK, that's just Too Much Information for me. TMI. How can I ever look at a Hershey bar the same way again?

You know who else shares Too Much Information with us? The airline industry. I remember when the media was full of reports that American Airlines were going to charge passengers $8 for a blanket. This would be the next chapter in the continuing saga of the industry's financial woes and how they struggle to find new ways to nickel and dime their customers in order to stay afloat during these difficult, difficult times.

For example, during the past few years, many of the airlines either stopped providing in-flight meals or charge anywhere between five to ten bucks for one. In 2008 US Airways announced a $25 per checked bag fee. Another airline I recently flew offered a premium seat, which was nothing more than a seat a few rows ahead of me, for an extra thirty bucks. Southwest (et tu, Southwest, et tu?) added a "priority boarding" fee, which allows ticketed passengers the option of getting on the plane approximately three minutes and twelve seconds faster than if they were to just hang around for regular boarding. And now this American Airlines thing.

C'mon guys. We don't need to know about your revenue

woes any more than we need to know that Hayden Panettiere recently reconciled with her ex-boyfriend. We don't care. It's TMI. Don't you get that? If not, then maybe you should listen to a few smart business owners I know who do.

Because these guys find ways to get additional revenues from their customers without turning it into a mass media event. They would never make public announcements or advertise these actions like the airlines do. It's just Too Much Information. It's like finding out that Tom Cruise will soon be making Mission Impossible 5. No one cares. And it's a perfect example of why so many small firms are run better than larger corporations. So to the guys running the airline industry with all their MBAs and other degrees, let a few of us business owners please offer you some pricing advice.

For starters, don't bring attention to your prices. Just bake in the extras. For example, we used to break out all the individual costs of the software products we sold - licenses, maintenance, support, shipping, handling, taxes, etc. All that did was open up a can of worms. Some customers would want to negotiate individual line items. It was a headache. So now we include all the costs as one number. Some of our overhead is included in handling so we spread that amongst all of our clients. US Airways, you've got computers, right? Figure out what these extra bags are costing you, build in a little profit margin and then include it in your pricing. We don't need to know any more than that.

Here's another crazy idea. Reward us. A friend of mine, John, runs a landscaping business and often gives stuff away for free to his best customers. Sometimes he throws them a fall cleanup on the house. Or he has one of his guys fix a drainpipe or gutter at no extra charge. Of course he always lets the customer know that he did the work at no charge. Now THAT's a good thing to advertise. Kind of like the free promotion those warm-hearted celebs got when they so graciously appeared on that Haiti fundraiser, during prime-time, in front of hundreds of millions of potential buyers of their products. Good people. Good promotion.

For John, giving away stuff creates a lot of goodwill. And keeps his good customers coming back. So here's a good idea, British Airways – before charging me extra for a "premium seat", how about just moving me to that seat at no extra charge as a little thank you for using your airline four times a year to drag my screaming kids over to London to see my in-laws, OK? You'll get more long term revenues out of me that way. Want me to have John give you a call and explain how this is done? Geez.

Andrea, who runs a fifty person printing company does the opposite of John, but with similar results. When she quotes a price to a customer she's got a special line item entitled "AF". The second letter stands for "Factor". And the first letter? Well, what do YOU call those customers who you hardly see, but when they do crawl out of the woodwork with a small order, their complaints, requests and demands create a lot of unnecessary work? Ah-hah, now it's starting to make sense. Andrea charges these people more. So Southwest, rather than charging a lame "Priority Boarding" fee, how about putting technology to work to find those similar high maintenance customers and up their pricing a mere ten or twenty bucks? What, like you don't know who they are? Oh yes you do. We all know who these customers are.

And American Airlines…believe it or not, I think you guys do a great job. I'm a frequent flier of yours. So instead of announcing a lame $8 per blanket charge, why not instead promote your frequent flier and "Business Advantage" plans instead, both of which are excellent. And one of the advantages of using these plans could be "discounts" off of your pricing. Let the non-frequent guys pay the extra cost somehow. Give us a break. I signed up as a "Preferred Customer" at the sushi restaurant down the street from me and instead of being told that the price of a spicy tuna hand-roll is going up a buck next month I instead get a coupon emailed to me offering a 15% discount on dinner. I feel appreciated. I keep coming back. I buy more spicy tuna hand-rolls. Get it?

And to the entire airline industry please, why not give Mobito Electric a call. Or A&A Signs. Or Jamestown Gaskets. I've changed these companies' names for purposes of this column. But they're all real and they all have this astonishing thing: a price list. This way your customers know what the published prices are for all services and products. These prices can include all of those extra fees you like to charge. Then let the travel services negotiate from there. Believe me, Mobito Electric doesn't charge a customer $50 to replace an outlet and then $250 to the customer next door for doing the same thing.

Did you know that former New York Governor David Patterson had been unfaithful to his wife and used both cocaine and marijuana? Did you know that Brad and Angelina were together (and shared a very loving kiss) at the Superbowl? Or that Heinz has developed a new and improved ketchup packet that solves all of the problems that the old one had? Do you care? Of course not. It's TMI. Run an airline? Want to charge an extra fee? Ask a smart business person how they would do this. If you do it right, we should never even know about it.

It's Time For A Timeshare

It's not a crock. It's not a scam. It's actually become OK to own a timeshare. And a few smart business people, like my friend Fred, have figured out a few good ways to turn this little purchase into some business benefits.

A quick review: a timeshare is generally a one or two bedroom apartment in a resort that you can "buy" in units or weeks. You can use it or trade it in.

You can get into a timeshare for less than $10,000. In fact, Fred bought his for around half that. He had the choice of lots of one-week deals around the world. He used a little outfit called The Holiday Group (www.holidaygroup.com) but you can find many other good companies that resell timeshares too.

In the end, Fred settled on a one-week unit located in Hawaii. Here's the thing: Fred has no interest in going to Hawaii. But he was told (correctly) that Hawaii, Florida and the Caribbean are the most popular timeshare locations around. So he figured owning a one-week timeshare would be a valuable trade-in.

Fred's timeshare is affiliated with RCI. RCI is owned by the Cendant Corp. that also owns Howard Johnson, Century 21, Avis Rent-A-Car and probably the Lincoln bedroom too. RCI's biggest competitor is Interval, another big-wig in the travel industry. RCI runs a big timeshare exchange system for its members — you can put your week up for exchange and grab someone else's timeshare for a week in another location.

Besides allowing exchanges, Fred gets deals on other vacation offers from RCI too. Beware though —these firms hire salespeople straight out of "Glengarry Glen Ross." Once on the phone they want to sell you time at their hotels, and other properties.

Also know that Fred has to plan way, way ahead to exchange his timeshare. I mean like two to three years ahead. Every time he does this he pays a fee. In fact, there are sometimes little transaction fees all over the place. This is in addition to the annual maintenance fees on the unit. These fees add up to a few hundred bucks a year, so Fred plays close attention.

Fred has yet to use his timeshare personally. He's got little kids. He has a business to run. He has no time for silly things like vacations.

But for his business … wow.

One year Fred donated the timeshare to a charity. It used it to raise lots of money for the poor and needy. This did not bring a tear to Fred's eye because, in actuality, Fred is a cold-hearted SOB. Rod Blagojevich is more of a humanitarian. However, he cried with happiness at the free publicity his business received.

One year, Fred used the timeshare as a grand prize in a sales contest. He offered the timeshare as an award for customers who bought the most of a new product line he was offering. For a few hundred in annual fees he generated many thousands in additional sales with a vacation week as bait.

Fred has given his timeshare away to employees too. Keeps them happy. They think he's a great guy. We know he's not. And to prove it he makes them pay their own plane fare. But it helps cushion the cost when you've got a free place to stay.

But here's the really good thing: not only can Fred use it himself once his kids are shipped off to reform school, but he can also resell the property too. Granted, he probably won't get the original five grand he invested, but maybe he can put a couple grand in his pocket after many years of use. Not a bad thing. With the stock market the way it is, Fred's used to depreciation.

Business owners need a break too! Go and buy that week in a vacation resort. Someday you may even find the time to use it. OK, probably not. But in the meantime, you can put it to work for your company.

Coupons For Your Customers Creates Cash

Aah ... the perfect restaurant. Alfredo's.

Alfredo's is located just a couple of minutes from my house. My wife and I go there frequently — a few times a month. This way we don't have to stay out too late. We can be back in time to relax and read poetry to each other.

The staff is friendly, but not too friendly. None of them sit in the booth with us when they take our order. They wear no flair. They're not chirpy or annoying. They don't address me by first name. They appear to have recently bathed.

The food is great. Fresh. Straightforward. Burgers. Steaks. Fish. Salads. Pasta. And always consistent. And the prices are reasonable. No $30 steak the size of a bagel that sits lonely on a plate without even a potato to keep it company. No $15 glasses of wine that clearly came from a box under the bar. No $4 cups of Maxwell House coffee served in 4-ounce dainty cups. Like I said... reasonable.

But it's the coupons. That's what makes a difference. All the stuff above is really great. But Alfredo's keeps us coming back with coupons. Because he's got a different approach to coupons. His approach is this: reward your customers first. Duh.

This isn't some kind of a Pizza Hut offer, where you buy 87 pizzas and on your next order you get free pepperoni. And it's not one of those buy-one-get-one free deals that are mailed by Val-U-Pak. These are all marketing gimmicks to attract new business from new customers.

Alfredo's goal is to continue bringing in business from his existing customers. A couple of times a year he gives out coupons only to customers. It's like... like... he appreciates us or something. I find this concept so refreshing, so unnerving, that I get chills just writing about it.

So a customer eats at Alfredo's, and after they pay they get a $10 coupon personally made out to them for the next dinner. That's all. Simple. Alfredo is saying "thanks for eating at my restaurant. We really appreciate you. We really want you to come back. Here's 10 bucks off your next meal." Refreshing. Unnerving.

Sure, we take the $10 off. But then, knowing we're getting a gift, we order another glass of that fancy wine that comes out of a real bottle, instead of a box. Or a dessert. You know, the ones with the flaming liqueur and all that kind of stuff.

Alfredo's cost is minimal. Our overall check still winds up being close to what it would've been without the coupon. But the 10 bucks keeps us coming back. We appreciate being appreciated.

Alfredo is a smart guy. He's not afraid to give stuff away to the people that are truly paying his bills. His loyal customers. We appreciate the offer and in turn give it right back to him.

Why is it that every deal, every offer, every coupon, has to be part of some marketing gimmick to attract new customers? What if we showed our existing customers how much we appreciated them? Maybe they would keep coming back and buying more. And maybe they'd be telling their friends about us, too.

The Wonders of Thank Yous and Free Stuff Too

Two stories, and both involve takeout.

A few months ago my wife and I stopped by an Italian restaurant to pick up a takeout order. The restaurant was busy and things were running behind. The manager came out to see us, apologized, and then gave us a free glass of wine while we waited. This is a smart guy. We got our food after a 20-minute wait and then, intoxicated, I drove into a telephone pole. Just kidding. We made it home fine. And we appreciated the gesture. We've been back for more food.

A few weeks ago I stopped by a local Japanese place for takeout sushi. The owner, who must be at least 104 years old, couldn't stop thanking me. I lost track at 37 thank yous. And I was only in there for five minutes. He then topped off my order with a free serving of edamame and five more thank yous. Another smart (but kind of annoying) guy.

Now, here's my story with a recent client. No takeout food is involved.

They're using one of our software products for their sales staff. They've spent many thousands of dollars with us for training and other services. We set up a training morning for their sales staff. It went well. Unfortunately, one of their key guys couldn't make it because of a personal emergency. They wanted him to get trained but were already at their budget limit. I sent out our trainer for another half-day visit at no charge.

No, I'm not Santa Claus. I didn't send out the trainer

because I'm a nice guy. I'm a selfish penny-pinching bastard. I wanted to keep the client happy. Demonstrate some goodwill. Show them that I care enough. That way they'll keep coming back for more services and will give me more money.

Is the Italian guy some kind of a hero? No. He just didn't want a couple of pissed off customers telling their friends and never coming back. The two glasses of wine cost him about 50 cents (I saw the box it came out of). The return on investment by keeping us happy was many times that.

And what about the thank-you guy? God only knows what he's muttering about me under his breath. I could swear I heard the word "bald" but I just can't be too sure. In any case, his politeness and demonstration of gratitude affects me, the cynical penny-pinching consumer, even in this day and age. I hate edamame too, but don't have the heart to tell him. It's the thought that counts.

People like to get free stuff. They want to get compensated for their time. The dollars really don't matter as much as the intention. Once I actually got a free month of cable TV service after I screamed at some poor customer service rep in Bangladesh loudly enough about the constant problems we had. This is ridiculous. Customers shouldn't have to yell and scream. We should be told that someone cares about us. We should be appreciated. Why do all the NEW customers get the royal treatment?

Good business managers aren't cheapskates. We don't haggle over small dollars. We give stuff away for free when we know that the gesture will return more in the long run. We're not shortsighted. Think about that the next time you screw something up. Offer a credit, or some cash back or even a gift certificate. Not edamame.

Smart business owners know how to show our existing customers that we really care about them.

Why John Should Pick Up the Phone

John owns a 20-person software company. Real person. Real company. Names are changed.

A few months ago we bought his company's software, and there were problems. OK, no big deal. Sometimes there are problems with software. We called the company for support. Unfortunately, we weren't getting the support we needed. Things were taking too long. Questions weren't answered. It was becoming a problem. In exasperation, I asked to speak directly to John. I was forwarded to his voicemail. Guess what message I received.

"Hi, this is John. I'm away at a conference this week with limited access. Please leave a message and I'll try to get back to you when I return." Limited access? Away at a conference? What, so like this conference is in Algeria? In the desert?

I have a friend who runs a law firm. When he goes on vacation, he likes to get completely out of touch. "I'm on vacation, man," he says to me, implying that I just don't get it. "When I'm on vacation I don't like to be disturbed."

What is this? Doesn't like to be disturbed? Smart managers don't do this.

This is the 21st century. If you own a business, this is what you signed up for. You're supposed to be disturbed. That's why you're making the big bucks.

Like it or not, technology has made it much easier to

stay in touch. So that's what smart people do. Take a look at all the 20-somethings today. These guys are used to having a cell phone glued to their ear. They're getting messages from everywhere. They're twittering away while driving. They're accepting RSS feeds while playing Frisbee.

These guys get it. And these are the guys who will be running their own companies before you know it. Some already are. They're already competing with you. And uh-oh... responding better, too.

Being accessible isn't just about better customer service. No one says you should be receiving messages day and night from customers who want to talk directly to the boss. Being accessible is also about your employees. Helping them do their jobs. Making them know that if they need to reach you they can. Wherever you are.

For example, sign up for Google Voice. Google Voice is free. You assign your cell phone voicemail to this service (don't worry, it's very easy to cancel). When a caller leaves a message, you get a text message alert. But that's not all. The text message also transcribes the voice message to words. Not perfectly. But good enough. The price is right. And you're in touch. Oh, and the voicemails get emailed to you or can be downloaded. This way you can keep a record of the voicemail on your computer, or just forward it to the right person to handle.

All of the major instant messaging services can be configured to send and receive messages from your cell phone. If an employee needs a quick answer, then you can provide it. Boo hoo that your little scuba expedition is interrupted for a few minutes. This is your business, dude.

You've also earned the right to invest in a decent smartphone. Get an iPhone or a Droid.

If you need to pull in a few employees for a call, then use Freeconferencecall.com. Yes, it's free. And it works. You can have a hundred people on the call at the same time. Your calls can go up to six hours.

Try remote collaboration services like GoToMeeting.com or GoToWebinar.com. These services tie-in phone calls and allow you to bring together customers or vendors from all over into one meeting room over the Net. This stuff works too.

You're not there, but that doesn't mean you're not accessible. Good managers know that this excuse just doesn't cut it anymore.

For God's Sake Don't Fire Your Customers

I was reading a book the other day by one of those business gurus. You know the kind. All fired up. Poofy hair. Loud voice. His thing is telling his audience to "fire your customers." Oh boy.

This guy is totally out of touch. He makes his income by selling books written at a fifth-grade level to over-eager business types. He gets paid $25,000 to appear at sales conferences, punch his fist in the air and cry out to his hungover audience "Fire your customers!" He sells tapes and videos on QVC to his legions of fans. Every year he comes up with a new catch phrase. What's next? How about "Castrate your employees!" Or "Behead your suppliers!" That could play well in Baghdad, I'm sure.

The poofy hair guy doesn't understand this basic fact: good business people don't fire their customers. We worked too hard to get them. We need the next order from that customer. We need his next check. Every dollar counts. I'd do business with Satan himself if the price was right, and I'd sleep like a baby that night, too!

So would my friend Greg. He runs a little printing company which grosses about $2 million to $3 million per year. Greg's got a few presses and a couple dozen employees. He deals with a lot of jerky customers. But he doesn't fire them.

Many of his customers have high demands and higher expectations. They have no patience. Turnaround time is short. Greg's competition is breathing down his neck. His margins are tight. Too much ink, and he loses money on a job. One bad machine part, and he's a day behind schedule. His pressman calls in sick, and Greg's up the creek.

Greg's got some customers who understand this, and others who don't. I guess the customers who don't are the ones the poofy hair guy is telling us to fire. But Greg's not about to fire anyone. Why? Because that customer's going to have someone print his latest catalog and Greg wants the work. But even Greg, like me, has his price. Remember Andrea from a few chapters back? She had a 'special' charge for those 'special' customers. A few years ago Greg came up with a little calculation for those special, pain-in-the-you-know-what customers too.

He calls it the PIA Factor. Greg doesn't fire his customers. He needs his customers. Even the pains-in-the-you-know-whats (PIAs).

Greg has created a very special row in his Excel spreadsheet when estimating jobs. That line is the PIA line. It's a very subjective number that figures into each of his quotes. It comes from years and years of dealing with PIAs.

When Greg estimates a new job he very carefully figures in inks, paper, other materials, press time, labor time, overhead, shipping and all the other costs he can think of. Then he adds in his secret ingredient. The PIA Factor. Is this customer a jerk? A PIA? Does Greg cringe every time he calls? When he sees this customer, does Greg have an overwhelming urge to punch him in the face?

All of this is included in The PIA Factor. It's judgmental, and it changes every time. But it's the price Greg needs to do business with this customer.

Need an example? OK. The PIA Factor for doing business

with Peyton Manning would be very low (he seems like a nice guy). For Donald Trump, high. Nicole Kidman: low. Rosie O'Donnell: high. Regis Philbin: low. Simon Cowell: high. Make sense?

Unlike what the poofy hair guy recommends, Greg doesn't fire his customers. He just changes the PIA Factor. A customer shouldn't be fired. They should leave on their own. Who are we to turn away work? We need every penny we can get.

Now put together a list of your customers. Decide which one needs to be paying you more. You already know who they are. Some may decide to leave, once you raise prices. But others may very well stay, and you'll at least feel like you're getting some compensation for the grief.

The Immaculate Reception

What's your favorite all time Super Bowl moment?

Was it Roger Staubach's "Hail Mary" pass to Drew Pearson? Or James Harrison's 100 yard touchdown run in Super Bowl 43? How about Bart Starr's famous quarterback sneak in the 1967 "Ice Bowl"? All of these were classic moments. Mine? By far it was "The Immaculate Reception."

But no, not the one you're thinking about. Not the play where the Steelers' Franco Harris took a crazy bounce off a defender and ran it in for a winning touchdown as time expired. That play was pretty cool. But I'm thinking of a different kind of Immaculate Reception moment. And it had nothing to do with the Super Bowl. Or football for that matter.

That moment occurred just the other day at a prospective customer's office. And it was quite thrilling. I walked in through the front door. I was greeted by a professional, cheerful person behind the front desk. My coat was taken. I was made to feel welcome. I was directed to a clean waiting area with a TV and free coffee. I even helped myself to a mini Snickers bar. It was, for me, an Immaculate Reception. And way better than some lucky catch made by a football player.

Look, I'm no expert in football. I graduated college in 1986. I worked for a big, international accounting firm for almost nine years. Eventually I started my own company. Am I an expert in accounting? No way. In fact, even although I'm a Certified Public Accountant I'm really not a very good one (for me, if it was close enough, it was good enough...not exactly stellar credentials of a good accountant). Am I a tech genius? Nope. A master at sales? No.

If anything, I'm an expert at reception areas. If you don't get it right there...well...it doesn't bode well for what's behind the next door.

I've been to hundreds and hundreds and hundreds of companies in the Philadelphia area (and quite a few outside the Philadelphia area). I know a good, organized reception area when I see one. And I've seen some pretty scary ones.

The worst ever was when I was still in public accounting. You would think that, working for a big international firm, I'd be sipping champagne and nibbling on caviar appetizers while waiting for my prestigious client to meet me in his lavishly appointed lobby. But I always had the misfortune of focusing on small businesses. One of those companies was the (now defunct) Futurama (I'm changing the name in case the company's owner decides to hunt me down and strangle me with one of the six gold chains he wore around his neck at the time.)

Futurama assembled furniture in one of the worst parts of North Philadelphia. Just walking from the chicken-wired-in parking lot to their front door was as risky as a stroll down any street in Baghdad during the Bush Administration. The worst part of this company's reception area was that there was none. You had to be buzzed in, hoping the front door (which was covered in graffiti) would be opened before someone stuck a knife in your back. Once inside there was usually no one to greet you. The first time I was there I wandered inside the building's dimly lit hallways, following the smell of cigarette smoke, until I find the company's 82 year old bookkeeper half asleep behind a metal desk and a filing cabinet that looked like a prop from the Dick Van Dyke show.

Reception areas are so important. Why do so many companies ignore them? Because they don't get it. Unlike true football fans, they don't appreciate the beauty of the Immaculate Reception. The good news? I've got a few recommendations.

Ever been to a customer's front desk and have to wave to get the attention of the receptionist because she's busy on the phone arguing with her boyfriend or absorbed in updating her latest Facebook status? Don't you love when she slides back the window like you're pulling up at a Burger King drive thru and instead of brightly smiling and saying "Hello, welcome to Barfco Industries, how can I help you sir?" you get a bored, wordless gaze until you're forced to say something first. Like: "Um...hello. I have an appointment with Mr. Jones?"

Which brings me to my first piece of advice.

Number one: if your receptionist is too thick to realize that her number one job is to greet people as they enter the company and make them feel like this is the greatest company in the world then fire her. Or him. Am I being sexist? Not really – I rarely see guys behind the front desk. Remember – I visit many companies too.

And while I'm on the topic of gender there's also the matter of appearance. I don't care what gender you are, most of us who visit companies want to see the same thing: a young pretty girl with a smile on her face. Or a relaxed guy, eager to help, with a smile on his face. Or an older nice looking woman with a smile on her face. Or a 94 year old with skin like an alligator....and a smile on her face. Notice a pattern? This is the first person we're seeing, the first impression we have of your company. We don't want to feel like we're a visitor. And we certainly don't want to feel like we're an intrusion. We want to be part of your family. We want to be doing business with you. It all starts with the very first words said to us as we enter your lobby. And whether or not someone's even glad to see us. Smile, for God's sake. I don't care what kind of day you're having. It's your job. And besides, research shows that it'll probably make you feel better too.

Number two: make your reception area easy to find. Why is this such a mystery? Over the past twenty years I've probably wasted two full days of my life wandering around office buildings, industrial parks and incubators searching for the entrance of the company I'm visiting. I've interrupted warehousemen smoking pot outside the receiving dock. I've stepped through puddles of toxic waste supposedly "out of sight" in the back of a machine area. I've tripped over four (and sometimes three) legged animals tied up behind a building. One time I got so lost I had to take a bus back to where I started. Actually, I'm not kidding about this – it was at a huge pharmaceutical company in north Jersey and I parked at Building 3 instead of Building 7. Who knew?

Have signs. Make it easy for your visitors. Remember, we're not going to pay attention to your instructions when you tell us on the phone – we're just too excited that you're actually going to let us visit. We're a little on edge. We're anxious about our meeting. Don't make us more anxious. Paint big red arrows. Cough up a few bucks and have a sign shop make signs like "Welcome – Office This Way." And don't forget the "Welcome." It's nice to feel welcome. It may sound corny. But it's nice.

Number three: clean up the area. Futurama didn't even

have a reception area (at least I couldn't tell if there was one whenever I tried to look past all the sandbags and anti-mortar artillery setup to defend against the surrounding neighborhood). A good reception area also tells a lot about a company.

For starters, upgrade your decor to say....post 1960's. Whenever I visit this one equipment manufacturer I know outside of the city I feel like I'm walking into an episode of Mad Men. "Mr. Draper will be down to see you in a minute" I expect to hear. C'mon guys...this shouldn't be an afterthought. A few nice sofas. A coffee table with a couple of Sports Illustrated and People magazines on it. A flat screen TV on the wall showing CNN is helpful to remind us how lucky we are not to be living in most other parts of the world. I like it when there's an interesting book or two left out too – sometimes it's a conversation piece ("Hey Barney, I didn't know you were into origami. So am I!").

A reception area should be friendly.   Comfortable. Welcoming. Up to date. Bright. Sunny. Cheerful.

Immaculate.

My favorite reception area ever? That would have to be at Bloomberg on Lexington Avenue in New York City. I was there once for a visit. From the minute you sign in you're directed by smart young future executives dressed in bright suits and laundered shirts to a waiting area with high ceilings that's situated right in the nerve center of their building. People are walking to and fro. Big TV screens flashed Bloomberg programs wherever you turned.   And, astonishingly, you're invited to help yourself to "refreshments" from this central kitchen area complete with Cokes, coffee, bottled water and (be still my rapidly beating heart) freshly baked cookies. I'm not sure I ever made it to the meeting I was supposed to attend. No matter – I walked out with a pocket full of loot.

OK, few of us are going to match that kind of reception area. And really, it's a little overboard. I'm happy if someone politely offers me a drink and a few of those mini Snickers from a bowl left out for guests. That's always a nice touch. Want to be a winner? You don't have to play in the Super Bowl. Just start with the reception area. The rest will fall into place.

The Next Mobile App Boom

The data is in: more people own a mobile device than a toothbrush.

This is not surprising of course. Everyone today has a smartphone or an iPad or something similar. Unfortunately, and I can only speak from personal experience, just about everyone I know mostly still use their mobile device like a toy. It's fun. You can make it burp and play scrabble with a friend or watch Iron Man on the train. And these are just the business people I know. Not that it's all fun and games. They do talk on the phone, send email and texts and check websites. Some of us are beginning to use our devices to pay our bills or buy something in a store. But the reality is this: for 99% of my clients use their iPhone, Droid or Blackberry is like a toy.

It's time to stop playing games. Smart, boring, conservative companies are getting serious about mobile applications. Slowly but surely, they're waking up to the potential..no, the need...to utilize these applications to develop more business and keep their customers coming back.

Of course, there are consumer-facing companies doing this every day. Like restaurant chain's P.F. Chang's new mobile application to help their customers find a location, make reservations and order takeout. Or Ally Bank, whose recent mobile offering lets their customers check account balances, search transaction history and transfer money between accounts.

Most major airlines allow their boarding passes to be sent electronically and a visit to Cinderella's Castle wouldn't be complete in this day and age without using Mobile Magic, Disney's official mobile app, to navigate its parks.

These are big, well-known companies creating cool apps for their customers. But other companies, both big and not-so-big, are quietly creating mobile applications too. Boring apps. But essential to the future of their businesses.

Home Depot's mobile application allows its contractors to order and pay for supplies from their phones. Pharmaceutical giant Merck released a mobile application to help people with type 2 diabetes. Chemical maker DuPont's mobile application gives service technicians refrigerant data on the go, enabling them to make quick and reliable system diagnostics. Dayton Superior , a provider of nonresidential concrete construction and paving products launched two free mobile applications to give their customers access to product and technical information on demand. Indianapolis- based Firestone Building Products Company, LLC, unveiled their own mobile application to help their customers (building owners, facility managers, roofing consultants) get quicker support. A mobile application software developer, Jomar Softcorp International Inc. is reporting a strong demand for its products amongst its manufacturing customers.

These companies know that mobile apps are not toys. These are tools. When it comes to mobile, we're just getting started. I believe that the mobile application industry is about to explode over the next few years. And it will be fuelled by millions of small and medium sized companies who will soon realize that having a mobile application is as necessary as having a phone number and a website to do business.

I can think of two of my own clients who are considering

this new reality.

One, a roofing company, wants to enable their customers to have immediate access to their customer service team when a truck is not onsite. They want their customers to be able to download information about the materials being used on the job, check on their job's progress, schedule service calls and look up their estimates and job totals. They want their guys in the field to use a table so that they can fill out work-orders, check their own schedules, get directions and make sure materials are in-house.

Another client of mine manufactures packaging materials. They want their customers to have mobile access so they can check on the progress of their jobs, order more materials and look up prior jobs. They also want to make sure their customers can get pricing quotes and place orders from wherever they are. Oftentimes their customers need more detailed specs about some of their products which they want to view from their smartphones or tablets too.

Think about it: we can all save whatever files, music, videos and photos for next to nothing on Amazon, Dropbox or other such services. Why can't businesses allow their customers to do the same? Why shouldn't every estimate, order and invoice be stored on a shared server? Why can't I view product specs, safety information and environmental releases about the products I've purchased? Why can't I immediately get my order history, job status and credit availability from a supplier? Why can't I get more personalized customer service? And why can't I get this from whatever device wherever I am?

And what do I get in return, as a business? By offering a free mobile application to my customers I'm (at least for now) differentiating myself from my competitors who aren't thinking this way. I'm saying to my customers: "Once you're part of my community you'll be treated specially. You can access us anytime from anywhere with our mobile app and get whatever information you need. Because we value your time." I can use the mobile application to provide special incentives to my customers. And even if the mobile application is not widely adapted, I'm at the very least giving some of my customers who prefer to do business this way a process that's desirable for them. It's all about choices. And ease. And time. Customers appreciate that.

There are plenty of software companies developing mobile applications and this trend will only continue to grow. But what's unique about today's development environment is that it's relatively inexpensive to have your custom mobile application written for your company. I tell most of my clients to expect to spend about $5,000-$15,000 in external fees. That's not a lot. Why so low?

Because there seems to be an unlimited amount of developers around the world who can be found on Craigslist, LinkedIn or through outsourcing sites like Elance, Guru and Freelancer. These developers have access to thousands of free programming apps to help them do their job quickly. Geography has been neutralized with our ability to monitor their progress and check their work using remote access and collaboration tools like Join.me, Gotomypc, Box and Basecamp. We don't have to worry about potentially compromising our networks either. Instead we can push data to hosting services like like Amazon, Rackspace and countless cloud infrastructure firms where our customers can access their data easily and securely. The most significant cost is the internal time that a business owner or key manager has to take to supervise the execution of the project, let alone designing the specs correctly after getting input from others.

The biggest decision is what platform. In the days of Windows dominance it was easy: you wrote (for better or worse) for Windows. Today you have to choose between the iPhone or Android (sorry, but unless something dramatically changes and despite the recent fanfare over the Blackberry 10 I don't see RIM being part of this discussion).

I prefer developing for the Android. I believe there are more tools available for the Android programmer and the system is more open. An Android application can be used on any device running that operating system (even Amazon's Kindle Fire) and you're not limited to just the iPad or iPhone. And I just like Google as a more business friendly infrastructure than Apple, who has a lot of consumer customers to worry about keeping happy. That said, I can't deny the popularity of the iPad among businesses. If budget allows, many of my clients may be forced to do what most big companies are doing for now: develop for both platforms.

But develop they must. Because every business should be thinking about building mobile applications today. It's not a fad or a passing trend. It's customer service.

The Secret to CRM

I learned the secret to a successful Customer Relationship Management system from a guy who sells seals.

No, not the kind of seals who balance beach balls on their noses for a treat of raw fish. Glenn's industry makes the kind of rubber and plastic seals that stop fluids inside of machines from leaking into unwanted areas. A veteran manager, Glenn has sold seals, gaskets, o-rings and other high performance parts that affect anyone who's ever flown in a plane, driven in a car or purchased a product that was made by a machine.

Glenn wouldn't seem to be a typical expert on customer relationship management. You won't see him presenting at the next CRM Evolution conference. He won't be writing about CRM in Forbes. He doesn't subscribe to CRM magazines or read the blogs. He's not familiar with, nor does he care about, the latest features available. He couldn't even tell you what 'social CRM' even means.

But Glenn knows more about CRM than most of the industry experts I know. And for most of his professional life he's used a CRM system every day. He relies heavily on his system. When Glenn changed jobs he called me. And this is what he said.

"Gene," he said. "I'm changing jobs."

He also said this: "I understand you sell a customer relationship management application called XYZ. I need to purchase XYZ software from you. I'm not saying XYZ software is the best. I know there are probably better. But that's what I've been using and I know it well. It does the job for me. And I'm going to need it at my next company. But here's the thing: I'm also going to need it to be setup exactly how I tell you. If you're willing to do that then I'm happy to work with you."

Glenn had a very simple objective for me. He emailed me four reports that he used at his last job. "Setup my system so I'm getting these four reports," he said to me. "That's all I want."

That's all? I asked him. You just want reports? What about all the other whiz-bang functionality today's awesome CRM systems offer? Like opportunity management and advanced forecasting? Or integrating it with one of your back end systems? Or setting it up so your staff can access it from their smartphones and other mobile devices? Or maybe just synchronize data? Or creating complex workflows to automate sales processes and improve productivity? And what about role based customization and security? And don't you want to produce mass communications via email and mail? What about all that great stuff?

"Nope," said Glenn. "Just give me those reports."

Glenn's new job wasn't that much different from his last. He somehow managed to avoid his non-compete agreement and switched companies within the same sealing industry. He came onboard to manage a team of fifteen sales guys. His team ranged in age from 25-60 years and brought with them all sorts of expertise. Some were better at closing deals than others. A few had very close relationships with large accounts. The younger guys were more technology-savvy while the older guys knew the business better. Glenn appreciated this. And he was willing to work along with all of them. He just had one big requirement: that they all use his CRM system.

There was no discussion about this. There was no evaluation. He didn't want to hear what his team "wanted" from such a system. Because he knew that everyone would want different things. The younger guys would want something web-based with a slick interface. The administrators would desire something that could eliminate data entry mistakes. The older guys, of course, would want nothing to do with it at all. With a fifteen person sales team there are always going to be fifteen different agendas. But to Glenn the only agenda that mattered was his. And the only thing that mattered to him was his reports.

That's because when you cut through all the hype, ignore all the marketing, push aside all the cool gadgets and gimmickry, a CRM system is just this: a database. That database may be sitting on your server in your office. Or it may be sitting on someone else's server somewhere in "the cloud." But that's about all that's really changed in the past twenty years. The fundamental part of CRM remains the same: it's all about the data. And really smart sales managers know that the best use of these systems is using the data to manage their sales groups.

So I set about constructing the four reports that Jim uses to manage his sales team. And I found that these reports were not very difficult at all.

His first is a Sales Pipeline Report. This report lists every "warm" sales opportunity his group is working on, with information about the prospect, the last action taken and the next action scheduled. The second is an Open Quotes Report.

This lists all outstanding quotes, the dollar value of each quote, the probability of closing and the age of the quote. The third is a Summary Activity Report. This is a chart showing how many calls and appointments were made by each salesperson during the past week and how many are scheduled for the upcoming week. And the last report is a Detailed Activity Report. This is the backbone to the Summary Activity Report and displays a line item detail of every call and appointment made (and scheduled to be made) by each salesperson, what was last discussed and what next action has been scheduled.

Every good sales manager knows these reports. But these reports are not the be all and end all. It depends on the company, the industry, the products...and how the manager runs his team. Some sales managers I know use completely different reports. One client of mine relies heavily on a weekly Leads Report, which shows what leads came into the company and from where. Another sales executive likes to read what he calls his Batting Average Report, which summarizes both closed and lost sales and calculates a won/lost percentage. This is all good stuff.

These reports are, of course, sortable. This way Glenn can list his open quotes from oldest to youngest so that he can figure out why those older quotes are still hanging around. And these reports can be, of course, filtered. Because Glenn may only want to zero in on the activities of a certain salesperson, or a certain region. Glenn doesn't like to spend that much time on the guys who are making quota, or doing what he expects them to do. He tends to focus on the guys that are falling behind.

Glenn's an experienced sales manager. As a manager he's responsible for the success of his group. To do his job in the eyes of his bosses he needs data. And he's learned this about CRM: the secret to a good system isn't wizardry. It's just having good data.

When I was hired by Glenn he gave me very simple, clear directions. "Install the XYZ software," he instructed. "And setup my reports. Create whatever fields need to be created so I get my reports. Train my guys to do whatever they need to do so that I can get my reports. Do not teach them anything else. Do not do anything else. When I am getting my reports then I will be happy and I will pay you. I may even be willing to discuss doing more things. As for the guys doing the data entry, let me worry about that. They'll do it. Or I'll find someone else who will." Harsh, maybe. But in 2012 this is what successful sales managers do. And successful companies know that CRM systems are not an option. It's part of the salesperson's job.

Getting More Production

From Your People

Secrets And Bonuses

Everybody has secrets.

J. Edgar Hoover used to keep his enemies' secrets in his FBI files by day and then sometimes secretly wear women's clothing at night. Our President has been known to secretly smoke cigarettes. I've always had a secret crush on Katie Couric. Well, now you know.

Kurt's got some secrets too. No, he doesn't wear women's clothing at night ("makes my legs itch"), drink too much alcohol, smoke cigarettes or lust after Katie Couric ("too annoying").

Kurt's secrets lie in his financial statements. No, he's not hiding anything illegal. He just doesn't want people to see how much or little he's making.

"This is nobody's business," he told me a few years ago. And he was right. One of the benefits of being a business owner is that you can fly under the radar and not have many others know all about your business. Our secrets are our secrets.

But times change. J. Edgar Hoover died and his enemies eventually disclosed his secrets. And when Katie Couric winks at me from behind that anchor desk I just want to shout out my secret feelings for her to the whole, wide world!

But enough about Katie. This is about Kurt. And for Kurt, what changed was the loss of a big customer. It's caused him to reveal his secrets. Share his financial statements. Particularly with his employees. Why?

"To keep them employed," he said. Kurt needed to come up with better ways to pay his people. So this smart business person sacrificed secrecy for a bonus plan. It turned out to be a great decision.

As revenues slowed, Kurt found it tougher and tougher to pay his employees. He was able to lay off a few of the nonessential people. But he didn't want to part ways with so many of the valuable people that helped him grow his business. People that he trained and who knew the company's operations as well as he did. People that would be busy once the economy began picking up again. So he decided the fair thing to do was to tie their compensation in with his company's profits. If they all worked hard and succeeded, they'd get more money. If the company didn't do as well, nobody (including him) did as well.

At the start of the year, Kurt determined he would allocate 30 percent of his profits to his employees for the next year. Not sales. Profits. He did the same thing in the following year too. Share the profits like this? What is he, some kind of a milquetoast socialist?

No way. Like me, Kurt's a capitalist and a red-blooded male through and through. Sure, he's not a big fan of Katie Couric. But he's mentioned Barbara Walters to me more than a few times.

Of the profit share, Kurt equally split the 30 percent among his four departments: operations, sales, service and financial. And then he let competition take over. He allowed his managers to grab the money and decide who, if any, in their department were to receive the bonuses. Including themselves. This gave the managers full discretion to reward those employees that they felt deserved the most. Some managers based this decision from formal employee reviews with goals and objectives. Others were more discretionary. Kurt didn't mind.

91

So why shouldn't the managers just grab it all? Well, Kurt always had the final say. Each manager submitted to Kurt their proposed split of the profit share along with explanations why. And Kurt could override these decisions if need be. So much for socialism.

Kurt didn't stop at the 30 percent profit share. He took another 10 percent of the profits and made a matching contribution to the employees' 401(k) plan, based on the bonus they received from their manager. That little extra, of course, only went to those employees who participated in the plan. This is Kurt's little way of saying "thank you for putting money away for your retirement so you won't come to me with your hands out when you turn 59."

Kurt's bonus plan worked. His employees, now fully vested in the company's profits, were motivated to see the company do well. They understood that the opportunity to get a year-end bonus was fully in their hands. They knew they had to please their own department head, as he or she would be making the bonus recommendation. Even participation in the company's 401(k) plan picked up as more employees wanted to take advantage of the extra company match Kurt was making at the end of the year.

Kurt plans to continue this arrangement, even as he inevitably brings in more customers. Some economists are warning that too much liquidity in the system could cause potentially high inflation.

Kurt plans to use this as a hedge — keeping raises as low as possible and offering employees the opportunity to make more money through the bonus plan.

Does a 40 percent profit share sound like a lot? "Not to me," says Kurt.

The generosity of this plan is returned by his employees' loyalty. Not that they're so in love with Kurt. It's just that it's tough to leave a job that pays so well for somewhere else.

Kurt found that paying his people well kept them working hard and productive. Penny pinching just to save a few bucks here would cost him way more in the long run.

The downside? "They get to see everything," Kurt says. For a business owner considering such bonus sharing, you better be prepared to let it all hang out. Kurt's beloved personal, private, only-for-his-eyes secret income statement suddenly became public info for everyone to see.

So do you have any secrets? A little pot smoking in your past? A dent that you put in someone's parked car that you never reported? A penchant for watching "iCarly"? Maybe you can hide these things. Maybe you can't. But if you're going to put in place a profit sharing plan like Kurt's, get ready to share your finances with all those around you.

When Siblings Don't Pull Their Weight

This is a true story about two brothers and their sister at Grundy Manufacturing. They'd rather not reveal real names--you'll see why shortly--but they want to spare thousands of other family businesses the same pain they endured.

Soon after the threesome bought the company from their father, a disturbing pattern emerged: Big Brother wasn't doing his fair share. He came into work late and left early. He shuffled papers on his desk. He talked to his friends on the phone. He played a lot of golf.

This went on for nearly five years. Resentment grew among the two other siblings. The final straw was when Big Brother disappeared for two days on a "customer golfing trip"--the customer being a fraternity brother from college and their two wives.

Fed up, the kids sought legal counsel. "Law firms face this issue all the time," says Joel A. Rose, a compensation advisor to law firms for 25 years. Rose's advice: "You must separate equity from compensation. Then agree on a quantifiable method to distribute the profits each year."

In Grundy's case, each of the siblings owned a third of the company. There's always been a buy-sell agreement in place, but no one had the stomach to trigger it; Mom and Dad would have been heartbroken if a dispute broke out. They let Big Brother keep his stake but, as law firms do, they tied his salary to performance.

Most law firms pay partners based on their clients' worth to the firm, net of expenses. At the close of the accounting year, each partner's annual billings are tallied and netted against the chargeable time incurred and amortized overhead. But there are also partners who don't bill as many hours because they provide other valuable services to the firm, such as overseeing employee training, research or administrative functions.

Grundy had a similar problem. Little Brother ran sales; Sister supervised operations in the plant; and Big Brother was responsible for all things administrative and financial. The challenge was not just how to deal with Big Brother's fecklessness; it was also how to fairly compensate all the partners, even though only one of them was generating sales. How to craft a compensation plan to account for all of those intangibles?

First step, they surfed websites such as Salary.com, Salaryexpert.com and Payscale.com to compare payment schemes for similar positions within their industry. They discovered that senior operations and financial people made about the same, while the senior sales and marketing people were paid about 25 to 45% more. They all agreed on set salaries based on their titles, position and this benchmark data. Little Brother, the sales guy, would pull down $150,000 while Big Brother and Sister made 25% less, or $112,000. (Total take for the three of them: $374,000.)

As for profit sharing, earnings were initially divided up among the owners based on their percentage of compensation. So, Big Brother, who was paid 30% of the total compensation ($112,000/$374,000) was entitled to 30% of the profits, too. Why initially? Because the profit-sharing breakdown was only a starting point.

At the beginning of the year, the siblings agreed on 10 annual objectives that each would undertake. For example, Little Brother agreed to land a certain number of new customers and implement a new sales tracking system. Sister would reorganize the warehouse, cutting two employees and training the production staff on a new piece of equipment. Big Brother reluctantly accepted the challenge of finding ways to cut freight expenses by 5% and choose a better health insurance plan.

The siblings drew against estimated profits throughout the year. Like a law firm, net earnings were distributed in January. (They held cash in reserve and leaned on a working capital line of credit.)

Here's the rub: Each missed goal translated into a 10% reduction in that person's cut of the profits, with the rest distributed equally among the two other siblings. Big Brother didn't like this arrangement, of course, but with only one third of the partnership vote, he didn't have much choice.

It turns out that adjusting the compensation structure was the best move the siblings ever made. The company thrived during the recession. Big Brother's performance has improved ... well, marginally. But that's OK. He's fine with his salary, his equity and his relatively small cut of the profits. Better yet, his disgruntled siblings now feel like they're getting paid what they're worth.

A Business Person's Community

Max is not a social kind of guy.

He's at work every morning by 7 and, if things are going well, he's back at his house around dinner time. He never answers the phone at home because he's on the phone dealing with people all the day. "And besides," he says. "If I wanted to be talking to someone I'd be calling them." He avoids his neighbors. He doesn't go to church, although he does admit to sometimes being hypnotized by Joel Osteen. He limits his extracurricular activities to watching his kids play soccer and going out to dinner with his wife.

But Max isn't a complete recluse. He's involved in a special community that no one in his family knows about. It's online. He visits it late at night. In the privacy of his den. When everyone's asleep.

He's got secret friends on this online community. They share intimate stories. They chat. They fantasize. They dream. Max looks forward to the time he spends with his online friends.

Want to get hooked up like Max? Want to meet people from all sorts of interesting places? Want to share your deepest secrets with strangers? Oh, yes. I know you do. You want to, don't you?

All right, calm down. It isn't what you're thinking. Max belongs to an online community for business owners. And trust me, it's about as sexy as watching C-Span. But if you're like Max, then getting free advice and information from other business owners and experts should be enough of a turn-on.

Max's online community isn't like Facebook. There are no stupid teenagers posting photos of themselves yukking it up with their BFFs. There're no stupid twenty-somethings pretending to be teenagers.

Instead, there are forums on small business issues with thrilling topics like taxes, technology, sales and marketing and the law. On these forums business owners like Max post questions about everyday business stuff. How does one pay a new salesperson? Would this marketing idea work? How come my computer keeps crashing?

There are experts too. CPAs, attorneys, advisers. Many of the online business communities bring in these specialists to field specific questions, write articles and offer their genius for free. Some of the best of these communities are free. Two popular ones are sponsored by Bank of America (www.smallbusinessonlinecommunity.com) and Intuit, the maker of Quickbooks (community.intuit.com). The sponsors at both of these sites pretty much take a back seat and don't shove their products down your throat. They're just trying to position themselves as "small business friendly". Whatever and hooray for them. As far as Max is concerned, both sites are free and well trafficked.

What does Max like best about his online business community? Anonymity. He can share the most confidential information about his business without fear of competitors or other evil-doers.

The worst part? Sometimes the advice he gets isn't always right. I guess this community is no different from any other!

Hire a Shrink, Make More Money

Adam sees a psychiatrist.

No, it's not because he's a Miami Heat fan. Or that he thinks Carrot Top is a funny comedian. These are certainly reasons why someone should see professional help. But these are not the reasons that Adam goes.

Adam, by all respects, is a pretty normal guy. He's been married 15 years. He's got three kids. With his sister, he helps run the family business -- an 80-person food distribution company. Adam drinks beer and likes to fish. Actually, Adam's not crazy at all. So why does he see a psychiatrist?

"For one hour a week," he told me the other day. "I do nothing but talk about myself. That's worth the $150 I pay."

I thought about this for myself.

Why would a penny pincher like me spend a $150 an hour to lie on a sofa and talk to a guy who looks like Bob Newhart about my problems? Do I really need to go into that time when I was bullied at recess or had my swimsuit pulled down in front of the entire 11th grade? If I can't eat my dinner unless I've first cut up all my food does that mean I should be seeing a psychiatrist too? Or that if I don't put on my clothes in a particular order each morning I have to start over again? Is this an issue?

"Dude," Adam said to me, backing away. "I just like to talk through my stuff with a guy. You, on the other hand, are a complete psycho." And he turned and ran.

Well, my own issues aside, I can see why Adam does what he does. Everyone makes demands on us from morning until night. A good business person seems to be constantly challenged with balancing work and family, employees and customers, vendors and contractors. Making our spouse happy sometimes feels like a full-time job. Making some of our customers happy seems next to impossible. How do we keep it all together?

Adam's found a way that works for him. He's not seeing a psychiatrist because of some doctor's orders. To him, it's a business expense. In fact, he told me that he charges the cost through the company's books as a consulting fee. I'm not sure if that's truly a tax deduction, but considering my own experience with consultants, I can see where he'd argue that there's little difference. In any case, I'll leave that decision to his accountant.

Does Adam's psychiatrist give him business advice? Marketing strategy? New product ideas? Not likely. In fact most of the psychiatrists (and psychologists for that matter) that I know can barely make their own coffee, let alone make real world decisions. But as trained professionals, they are definitely qualified to act as sounding boards and thought provokers for their clients.

"And here's another good thing," Adam said after he tentatively came back to talk to me a few days later. "My psychiatrist has no agenda. He's independent. He's not trying to get on my good side. I pay the guy, he listens to my problems. He talks them through. And when the hour's up we part ways and I don't see him again until the next session."

So is Adam a little out there? Well, clearly no more than me. But as a successful business owner, he definitely sees the value in getting outside help ... for his mind. It keeps him sane. It lets him vent. And he can return to his crazy life with a little more perspective.

Exit – Stage Left

Ryan Seacrest understands exit interviews.

Even those contestants on *American Idol*, who sing worse than I sing, were given a few minutes with the interviewer after their audition to have their say. Humiliated, disappointed, often angry, many of these people had no shortage of rebuttals about the process and, of course, the judges (particularly that very arrogant British one).

That's what the exit interview is all about. On *American Idol* it's entertainment. In a small business it's information. In both cases it's done to satisfy the organization, not the participant.

"So how did you think you did?" Seacrest innocently asked one 800-pound contestant after failing to win over the judges with her rendition of Madonna's "Like A Virgin."

"Oh," she replied. "Those judges don't know a talent when they see one. They rushed me through and didn't even let me finish!" Thank God for that.

Whether or not the judges were at fault, the *American Idol* audience is entertained and the producers get educated. Business owners can also get educated. And the good ones make it a point to conduct an exit interview with every employee leaving their company, no matter what the circumstances.

Sometimes an employee gets fired and sometimes he may leave on his own accord. But before he's out of there, sit him down in your office, close the door, and shine a bright light on him. Better yet, treat him to a beer or five or six, and have a nice little conversation about the circumstances of his departure.

Sorry, this isn't about the employee. Only someone as naïve as Ryan Seacrest could actually believe that the employee cares a thing about the company he's leaving. He's moved on already and thinking of the next job. As you share Jello shots, keep in mind that the goal here is to siphon off as much information about your company as you can before he's out the door, never to be seen again.

Now's the time to get the real dirt. Exit interviews are great for that.

Which employees are slacking and who's working hard? Is there ill will or rising problems that you don't know about? Any customer complaints buried under the rug? Hidden product problems? Who's mouthing off? Who's unhappy? Why are Anne and John taking so many lunch breaks together? A good exit interview can reveal a lot of potential issues that you might not have been aware of.

Exit interviews are a good place to look in the mirror too. Plied with the right questions and the right amount of alcohol, you may be able to get more honest feedback about yourself and the way you run your company from an ex-employee who's moved on, than from someone currently on your payroll. If you've got a thick skin, and most good managers do, then you can use this information for positive changes.

Exit interviews also show respect. Respect for the ex-employee and for your current employees. There's something to be said for a business owner willing to take time aside to sit down with someone who's leaving his company and give the employee the opportunity to speak his mind. Besides the information you'll hopefully use to improve things, there's no better way to end your relationship than on amicable terms.

And an employee's amicable departure is potentially profitable. The world's not such a big place and it's never a good idea to burn bridges. You may very well be seeing that employee again and he might want to come back to work, armed with intelligence from one of your competitors, more experience and a better attitude. At the very least he might want to pay for a new round of drinks this time.

Good managers do exit interviews. They don't let a person go without squeezing as much information as possible from them.

Seacrest ... OUT!

Getting Sick of Sick Days

An article in Inc. Magazine referred to a survey which reports that only a third of the people who call in sick to their employer are actually ill. This makes me sick.

I'm sick of employees who call in ill when they're not really ill. It's fraudulent. It's dishonest. It's stealing time away from the company. If that same employee were to take the equivalent dollars from the company's petty cash box he'd be fired on the spot.

I'm sick of experts telling us that sick people shouldn't work because they'll spread their germs among other employees and make them sick too. First of all, anyone with kids under the age of ten walks around in a perpetual diseased state anyway from all the bugs brought home from day care and school. We all just get used to the feeling. Secondly, I just don't buy that a "sick" employee can't take precautions to avoid contact with others that day if they're so mortally contagious. Finally, if it's that bad ... get a remote connection and work from home.

People in responsible positions don't take sick days unless they're getting surgery that day. CEOs, presidents, politicians, high paid actors, doctors, lawyers ... how often do they take sick days? Not a lot. Do they have healthier jobs? Better diets? Stronger genes? Of course not. They just know that they have obligations to meet and the sniffles aren't reason enough to blow them off.

I'm sick of human resource consultants coming up

with all of these "flexible" plans to "balance" work-life commitments and create a more "positive and happier" work force. Give me a break. Human resource people love complex plans that incorporate sick days, vacation days, flex time, and family leave absences. Why? Because it's job security for the human resources people.

The only good side is that they're so busy calculating the right amount of time off allowed by some overly complicated benefits plan that they don't have enough time to take a sick day either.

I'm sick of this whole "rolling over" concept too. You know, where you don't use your allotted days and they roll over to the next year? For a small business owner, this becomes an administrative nightmare. I've seen employees that have rolled over enough unused vacation days to take a year off.

What good does that do? If days aren't used, then just pay it out in cash and wipe the slate clean for next year.

I'm sick of requiring documents like doctor's notes when someone's out sick. Exactly when did kindergarten end? Why are grown men and women submitting forged doctor's notes to uncaring personnel clerks anyway so a checkbox can be marked? It's humiliating to those workers who actually have a legitimate excuse, and just gives another way for the slackers to grease themselves through the system.

Good managers don't buy into complicated sick day plans. Here's what I've seen works the best: you give employees a set number of days off and they can use it anyway they want. There's no differentiation between a sick day and a vacation day. It's just a day off. If a day off exceeds the number of days allotted ... there's no pay. If it becomes unreasonable, excessive, unproductive or just plain annoying then the employer has the right to terminate.

Extended illnesses? Special circumstances? Of course we're going to do the right thing. We know the big picture. We all want this relationship to work. We're business people and have much invested in our employees. Losing one is painful.

Are you feeling poopy-woopy this morning? Does your keppy hurt? Poor baby. Go ahead, take a day. We trust you. But act like an adult. Don't take advantage. Or you'll be out of a job.

Go Get It Yourself!

A smart person once said that children are best seen, not heard. Unfortunately, many of us feel the same way about our customers.

We love them, sure. Customers help us pay the mortgage (well, some of us) and buy a nice meal every now and again. And, of course, we want to provide the best service possible. But do we have to talk to them so much too?

Holding customers' hands can get expensive--especially if you have a sprawling customer base full of other small businesses.

Just ask Jeff Stibel, chief executive of Website Pros, a 700-employee company that provides Web site hosting, marketing and lead-generation services to more than 250,000 paying customers. How does Stibel keep his sanity? A bottle of Jack Daniels comes in handy. But mainly it's because he leans on the latest in customer self-service technology.

Self-service software lets customers create their own orders and check on their status--no human intervention required. Those that need instant, interactive troubleshooting without an extended phone call can use online-chat software. Other self-service tools include basic "how-to" and tech-support videos and articles--or something as fundamental as mapping software that offers driving instructions to your office. And don't forget "wikis"--online information repositories that can be shared and updated by customers.

Over the years, Stibel has spent in the "seven figures"

to buy or build plenty of customized self-service tools. The investment was worth every penny: "We estimate [our self-service tools] have saved us millions of dollars," he says.

Here's how: Say you're a Website Pros customer, and you need help setting up a new e-mail account, or you're getting an error message on the Web site the company is hosting for you. You could call the toll-free number--or you could go straight to the Website Pros site and click on the member sign-in tab.

From there, you'll be immediately bounced to a customer-support portal, where you'll be asked for a user name and password. From here, you can create a new order ticket, update an existing ticket, reset your password, request add-on functionality or search for relevant, helpful articles.

Anything you do is then passed through to the company's internal support system for processing, based on the issue you've raised. The system will automatically update you (and the relevant propeller-heads at the company) to handle the problem.

Of course, customers that want to speak to a human can always call the help desk (and get a neck cramp holding the receiver while they wait their turn). But more and more are choosing to take matters into their own hands online. Which brings us to the other great thing about self-service tools: They not only save money for companies, they keep customers coming back, because you've saved them time and aggravation.

Where do you find self-service tools for your business? A Google search on "customer relationship management" or "help desk" software will turn up scads of vendors. For more ideas, check out the Help Desk Institute too.

Remember: The squeeze is on--and managers have to find a way to get things done better and faster for less money. Self-service tools are a great place to start.

Not You, But Who!

I learned an important lesson a few years ago: If you shoot a non-paying customer in the face with a high-powered shotgun then you will make a big mess and almost certainly go to jail. So I decided not to shoot the guy who was stiffing me. Instead, I asked my bookkeeper Susan to politely call him and collect the money he owed us. It took a few calls, and a few more weeks. But Susan succeeded. I got my money. I avoided jail time. And a light went on.

From that moment forward I delegated all collection tasks to Susan. No longer did I feel bile rising in my throat every time a customer promised to pay and didn't. The nausea that hit me every week as I watched certain invoices creep past 60 days went away. Susan took care of these problems. And when she couldn't, we would unleash our collection attorneys — so the customer could at least be on the receiving end of a few threatening letters.

Susan followed up with those slow paying and deadbeat customers professionally, if not indifferently. And why not— it wasn't her money. She wasn't emotionally attached like I was. It was a job. And she does it well.

Because of her, my collections increased. My arguments with customers decreased. I began to lose weight. Hair started regrowing on my head. I got my first-ever varsity letter. Mary Jo agreed to go to the prom with me. I finally got accepted to State and plan to study law. My papa's so proud of me he let me use the Ford on prom night.

109

This isn't a story about collecting money. It's a story about getting someone else to collect my money. Business people that succeed do so because they delegate the things that they don't do well, or don't want to do. They do this so they can focus their efforts on the things that they do the best.

Bill manages his company's finances himself on Quickbooks. Joanne was up at 9 p.m. last night stuffing envelopes for a mailing. Jerry insists on calling on certain customers because of his long-term relationship with them.

These are not penny pinchers. They are cheapskates. These people are all wasting their time. Bill should pay a bookkeeper to do his books. Joanne should have a mailing house do her mailings. And Jerry should get off his high horse — he's not so irreplaceable. I'm sure his customers will cope if someone else in his office took their orders once in a while.

Life is short. Resources limited. Why are we doing things we don't like to do? Why are we doing things that we're really not so good at, instead of things that we're good at? Cheapskates continue to do things themselves. Good managers invest in others to do tasks for them.

Are CEOs of large companies doing their own bookkeeping or stuffing envelopes? They have people who do that for them. If they're managed well, the job gets done well. And the CEO can have more time to do other important CEO stuff.

Bookkeepers, sales people and telemarketers can be found on the web. And they don't even have to be local. There are remote connection tools that I've just discussed in previous chapters, and there are hosted phone systems like Virtualpbx. com and Grasshopper.com. We have intranets, e-mail, instant messaging and video conferencing. A contracted engineer can work from her house in Montana or a receptionist can be in Maine.

If you're not delegating because you don't want to spend

the money, then you're a cheapskate. But if you're investing in someone to do something so that you can do something else more productive and profitable then you're a smart business person. Finding the people is not hard. What's hard is changing one's mindset from a do-it-yourself small business owner to a profit-making manager.

Mark And Betty: A Penny Pincher's Affair

"It's scandalous," whispered one of Mark's employees to me. She was referring to her boss's relationship with Betty. "He's just using her for his own pleasure. It's disgusting."

Mark is a man. And he has his needs. He runs a ten person independent hardware store on a main street in a small town. He inherited the business from his father, who retired a few years back. He works hard and his hours are long. It's demanding, a thankless job. Mark employs about ten full time people who help him manage his stock and tend to the cash register. For a while, Mark's wife would help out with the bookkeeping and accounts. But then she had their first child and didn't have the time to devote to the store. And that's when Betty came into Mark's life.

"I've never seen anything like it, this carrying on," muttered Mark's cashier. "Mark's father would never have stood for this kind of behavior."

"Mark's a penny pinching business owner who puts in long hours and is struggling to survive against his larger competitors and a slow economy," his accountant confided to me. "Let the guy have some fun."

At first look, you wouldn't think that Mark and Betty would have a lot in common. Mark's in his thirties, in good physical shape, works out every day, and has a full head of hair. Betty, in her early sixties, could lose about twenty pounds, has two large corns on her feet, smokes like a chimney and stopped dyeing her gray hair soon after her sixth child was born.

But Betty and Mark have a special relationship. Only the kind of relationship that a penny pincher could appreciate. Betty does Mark's bookkeeping. She keeps his accounts receivable. She handles his cash receipts. And she arranges his files. What makes her so special to Mark? Is it that bloodshot look in her eyes? Her brittle fingernails? The way she snaps at young children?

"She's a temp," sighs Mark. "That's why I love her."

Mark hired Betty through a temp agency. He didn't take an ad out on Craigslist or Monster.com or the local newspaper. He didn't have to sift through hundreds of resumes sent to him by people from all over the world. He didn't have sit down through endless interviews with overqualified people desperately looking for a job, any job. He didn't have to worry about an applicant's qualifications, bookkeeping skills or prior employment history. His temp agency did all that.

The temp agency has their own pool of people for the kind of job Mark has. They're the ones who worry about finding these people, interviewing them, testing them, qualifying them and checking out their past experience and history of drug abuse. They're the ones who hooked Mark up with Betty. They're the ones who made this match that only some say could only have been made in heaven. Forget about eHarmony – Mark's temp agency was responsible for finding the love of his life.

That's not to say that Mark fooled around with a few others before finding Betty. Because he did. There was Rosie, the one who wore too much makeup and came to work late too many times. And Chloe, the young, dark haired beauty who did excellent work and was promptly dismissed within a day after Mark's wife dropped by the store on her way to the daycare center. And of course Gary, the mustached biker who quietly went about his business and then one day disappeared…never to be seen or heard from again.

But this wasn't Mark's problem. That's because he used a temp firm. Whenever a person didn't work out, they just sent another. And usually by the next day. Unlike before, Mark didn't have to pull out the old stack of resumes, or frantically call people on the phone, or place yet another ad and spend another few weeks looking for that special person again. Mark wasn't thrilled about the revolving door of temps he saw. But his prayers were one day answered when Betty showed up at his store.

"It was like a thunderbolt hit me," Mark fondly remembers. "I'll never forget the first moment we met. It was a rainy Tuesday morning. She looked so lovely in her dead husband's London Fog trenchcoat over a flowery housedress and black galoshes. And when she threw down her umbrella, lit that first cigarette and asked me to point her to the books and records I thought I would faint with joy."

There's no denying that Betty costs a little more. Mark pays about twenty bucks an hour for her services to the temp firm. But he considers that a bargain. He doesn't have to pay employer taxes or unemployment insurance. He doesn't have to worry about her vacation plans or her retirement plan. And, after overhearing Betty mention the size of the hemorrhoid she's been sitting on all day he's especially relieved to not have to think about what her health insurance is costing. All that's built into the rate. We all know how money can ruin a relationship. Because the temp firm worries about these things, Mark and Betty are free to enjoy themselves without being bothered about these everyday affairs.

Mark's a married man and a father of three beautiful children. But he's a man. And men have their needs. And Mark soon found himself drawn to Betty. He loved to watch her spittle as she told him his daily cash balance. He watched her lovingly as she barked on the phone at overdue customers

114

in her phlegmy voice. He looked at her shapely figure as she bent over to file away suppliers' invoices. Mark found himself falling more and more in love with Betty.

Things were bound to come to a head. And they did. After about four months of having Betty around the office Mark could stand it no further. He called up the temp agency and inquired about a long term relationship. And, like most good agencies, they were able to accommodate. Many agencies will let their customers hire a temp away full time if they've had them employed for a certain number of months. Others will charge a fixed fee, generally a percentage of their starting salary.

And so one day as he was closing up shop Mark approached Betty. He confessed his love for her. The way she chewed on her pencil while adding up the day's receipts with that one snaggly tooth of hers. The intoxicating smell of old pretzels and mothballs that emanated from her. He asked her to be his forever. He would handle things with the others. He would make a long term commitment. If only she would stay on at the store and do those things that only she knew how to do to make him so happy.

But Mark was in for a shock. Betty had a secret. She was seeing someone else. On the side. A graphic designer on the other side of town. She was doing his books too. And right under Mark's nose – on the days she wasn't at the hardware store. Mark couldn't believe it. How could this happen, he asked her? "Oh, a temp's gotta do what a temp's gotta do," she said, taking a drag from her cigarette and packing up her handbag.

Mark watched her hobble off to catch the bus. He'll get over this. Tomorrow's another day. And there'll always be cash to collect. And if Betty's not there to collect it, you can bet that Mark's temp firm will find someone else for him.

The Right Way To Interview

I've met a lot of successful executives who got C's in high school and drank their way through college. I've met a lot of smart people who worked their way up to senior management from lowly positions. Conversely, I've met a lot of dopes who went to Ivy League schools and worked at big corporations who, in my opinion, are less valuable than people making half their salaries.

Why? Because experience and academic qualifications matter…but not as much as we think. Good penny pinchers know that the best employees bring more important qualities to the table. Common sense. Work ethic. Reliability. A buddy who can get tickets for NCAA games. There's plenty of great people to hire out there right now. How do you know who's the best? It's all about asking the right questions at the interview.

So as a service to all of my fellow business people looking to hire someone in 2013, I've put together a list of eight key, completely legal questions you should consider asking if you want to quickly weed out the weaker candidates and find your stars.

1. Do you agree with hiring Mariah Carey to be on American Idol?

The objective of this question is to determine the applicant's common sense. And any applicant that thinks

Mariah Carey adds value to American Idol clearly does not have enough common sense to work at your company and should be disqualified. Everyone knows the show has jumped the shark since Simon left. Extra points to the candidate who admits to never watching American Idol at all.

2. Who is your favorite sports team?

Here, you're trying to establish the applicant's potential loyalty to your company. The answer has to be a hometown team. Even if the applicant grew up in Denver and lived in Philadelphia the past ten years, it says more about his character that he's still a Broncos fan instead of someone who just changes sides depending on where the wind blows. We want people that are loyal, that will stick with us through good times and bad. Except for Mets fans. Never, ever hire one of those.

3. What is your typical weekend schedule?

This helps you establish work ethic. If, like me, the applicant seems to spend her weekends chilling out, watching TV or drinking while driving then this must mean she's been working so hard during the week that she needs a good rest over the weekend to recharge. On the other hand, if an applicant claims that she spends her weekends helping the poor, jogging in the park and doing projects around the house it's clear that she's not expending enough effort at her job during the work week and should be disqualified.

4. Your wife wants to try that new vegan place and you want Outback for dinner. Who wins?

What kind of decision maker is this applicant? If the answer's Outback then disqualify him immediately. A guy that fights with his wife over where to have dinner is a guy with poor decision making skills. Doesn't he realize that once he walks in the door to his home he makes no more decisions? The right decision is to smile, eat a few veggies and pop in a Hot Pocket once she falls asleep.

5. Do you give to any charities?

This has nothing to do with an applicant's generosity. It has a lot to do with her income. Smart business executives love when employees give a lot to charities. The more they give, the more they'll need to earn so the harder they'll work. And if you can convince them to re-direct their charitable giving to the company's own United Way fund you can look like you're a real charitable guy by riding on their coattails. Charitable giving is a big thumbs up.

6. What kind of car do you drive?

If the applicant drives a Toyota then you'll need to disqualify. Who knows the effect on your health insurance? Who you really want is that guy who's stupid enough to lease expensive cars and trade them in every two years. Don't hire him if he's looking to work in your accounting department because this guy clearly doesn't know the first thing about personal finances. But he'll be so tied down to his car payments every month he'll be your virtual slave in return for his paycheck. Stick him in sales and push him hard.

7. What's your favorite Rob Schneider movie?

Your company depends on the quality of the service and products you sell. So if the applicant answers "Deuce Bigalow, European Gigolo" then hire that guy on the spot. Clearly this person knows quality when he sees it. If the answer is "The Hot Chick" then show him the door. See, I told you this wasn't so tough!

8. Which is more boring – dinner at your in-laws or your daughter's 5th grade graduation?

Here's the true test of honesty. There is no right answer here. Everyone knows both options are horrible. The in-laws are grating. The graduation ceremony is an exercise in rewarding mediocrity. Which one is worse? The key is the honesty of the applicant's explanation. Does he admit to once wanting to pour that boat of gravy over his mother in law's head? Or does he acknowledge that his yet-to-be-house-trained puppy is capable of graduating 5th grade at his daughter's elementary school? The more honest the response, the better the applicant.

Smart business owners know that hiring the right employee is not as tough as people make it out to be. It's not all about their education, or even their experience. It's all about whether that person will work hard, show up on time and fit in. Except if they're a Mets fan.

Happy hunting!

Keeping Expenses In Line Now

To Free Up Cash Later

Here's The Way To Get Yourself Some SWAG

What do Keanu Reeves, Leonardo DiCaprio and a small business owner named Jack all have in common? Let's see. Keanu and Leo are mega-rich. Jack is not. Keanu and Leo are both very good looking. Jack has a mole the size of a peach on his forehead. They both get a lot of action with the ladies. Jack has a wife named Dolores and a dog named Clete.

But, believe it or not, there really is something in common between these two Hollywood celebs and a smart business person. All three are experts at getting some SWAG. You don't have to be rich, famous or have a mole the size of a peach on your forehead. Just ask Jack.

SWAG means something like "stuff we all get" or "stolen without a gun." You know, freebies. And Keanu, Leo and Jack get a lot of freebies. Did they save a life? Help the poor?

Nah. In the actors' case, they just presented at the Academy Awards a couple of years ago. And for their efforts here's some of the things they got: A choice between a retreat to the Mayan Riviera or a Canadian ski vacation, (worth $2,500), a spa day at a resort in Manhattan ($2,500), an espresso machine and cups ($600), a vintage silk kimono ($500) and other stuff. By the way, I am not kidding here.

Jack did not present at any Oscars ceremony. However, Jack gets his SWAG from consultants and service providers who want to be hired by him. Oh, it's no silk kimono I'm sure, but the value of the services that Jack gets for free each year is pretty comparable to those Oscar gifts.

Take, for example, Jack's taxes. He's never entirely sure if his accountant is saving him as much as he can. So every few years Jack calls on some other accounting firms, tells them that he's considering a change, and asks for their comments on his returns. He always gets some interesting ideas. One firm recommended a creative way to save more taxes by deferring income. When he brought this idea to his current accountant they both agreed that it would be a good thing to do. He didn't switch accountants that time, but who knows about the next time?

Jack often gets free technology consulting advice too. Never completely satisfied with the people supporting his computer system, he often invites other competing information technology firms to come in, take a look at his setup, security, etc. and propose how to make it better. Times are tough and these service guys are hungry. He's up for making a change if the proposal makes sense. But at the very least he's getting some free advice on how to improve.

Is this ethical? Of course it is. Jack's a smart businessperson. He's not taking advantage. He's trying to keep his current service providers on their toes. He's giving an opportunity to another service provider to take the business away. And no matter what, he's getting good advice. Everyone's a grown-up here. If a competing firm doesn't want to take Jack up on his offer they're free to move on.

Now take a look at all the people and firms providing services to your business. Are they doing the best job possible? Are you getting the best advice out there? Are your insurance rates as low as they could be? Is your attorney keeping you up to speed on all the key issues that you should be thinking about? When was the last time your employee benefits were reviewed?

Yes, even YOU can be more like Leonardo DiCaprio! Get some SWAG in the form of free consulting. Beat up on your service providers. Come away with a few more ways to save a few bucks. Who knows, you might save enough to buy one of those vintage silk kimonos yourself.

Ask And Ye Shall Receive A Lower Price

I was never one for asking for a lower price ... until I found myself getting lower prices by asking.

The reality of doing business today is this: Everyone's got a price. If I told you to shed your clothes and go streaking across Fenway Park on a January Sunday you'd look at me like I were asking you to streak across Fenway Park on a January Sunday.

"Hmmph," you'd sniff. "Exactly what kind of a person do you think I am?"

But suppose I offered you a million bucks to do that (and showed you the cash).

If you're like me, then your greedy little mind would go into action, wouldn't it?

"Wellllll," you'd think to yourself. "That shoplifting charge was so long ago, it's probably forgotten. And I'll only get a fine and maybe probation. And no TV camera has powerful enough lenses to cause me too much embarrassment with that girl I recently met at happy hour. And it is a million bucks, isn't it. So why not?"

This is the same thought process that goes through the mind of any sales person when you ask for a lower price. Except for the shoplifting part (I hope). The point is ... everyone has his price. As a good negotiator, it's our duty to push for the lowest price possible by asking, asking, asking.

For example, you need to buy eighty cubic yards of industrial squash from that cigar-chomping guy near the airport, and he tells you it's ten bucks a yard. You can accept this price or come back and say it's too much. You need the industrial squash. But guess what? He needs the business. We all need the business. He'd love ten bucks a yard, but then again he'd love to be smoking a Cuban cigar instead of the cheap ones he buys at 7-11. Chances are he'll come down a bit. Multiply that bit times lots of yards over a period of time and this adds up.

My wife, the ultimate penny pincher, got two estimates for putting a carpet in our basement. The company she liked better quoted (of course) $400 more. Just by asking, they knocked $200 off the price. Wow. That paid for almost half of the damage their installers wound up doing to the entrance way.

Why should you always ask for a lower price? Because that's what your customers are doing to you every day, aren't they? I find it incredible, shocking, outrageous and downright insulting when, after clearly stating our hourly fee, a client asks for it to be lowered. How dare they! And of course ... I usually lower it. Why? You know why. I want the work. I don't want my competitor to get the business. I'd probably throw in a personal car wash to get the guy's business. What ... you're different?

Smart managers are not afraid to ask for a discount. No one expects you to negotiate a treaty with North Korea or haggle like an experienced merchant. But not paying top price is what profits are all about. Your job is to ask and take whatever you can. Just because you can afford the price doesn't mean you have to pay the price.

Ask. You will receive.

Gourmet Coffee Is A Waste Of Money

I like Starbucks. It's fun to go there and check out the people, get a high-speed connection, spend four bucks on a cup of coffee and even annoy the girl behind the counter by asking for a "small" latte instead of "tall." Gourmet, overpriced coffee has a place in our culture. But not in our offices. This is just taking coffee way too far. Let me explain.

I'm at a client the other day and he says, "Hey, Gene, would you like some coffee?" so I say, "Sure". What happened next occurred over a 15-minute span.

First, my client proudly shows me his new gourmet coffee machine and all its fine features. He has built a new room, complete with plumbing, to house it. My client is then forced to explain the elaborate procedure for making a gourmet cup of coffee after reviewing the reference manual and pointing my attention to a large poster board over the machine with a diagram of the coffee-making process. I am privileged to be able to choose from one of 15 gourmet coffee flavors. I can't really explain, but for some crazy reason I just wasn't in the mood for mocha-peanut-butter-and-jelly-supreme that day so I went with regular.

I proceed to pull the little container out of its specially designed display case and insert it into the gourmet coffee-making machine's specially designed slot. My client danced with delight in anticipation of what was going to happen next. I then push a button and stand there for 45 seconds ...

immersed in the flashes of blinking lights and gurgling coffee as the machine does its job.

Mercifully, and to my client's childlike glee, the gourmet coffee begins to dribble slowly into a disposable cup, its tepid stream ending when the cup is less than half full. The machine is kind enough to display the word "DONE!" to let me know that my gourmet coffee is now available to consume.

The craziness doesn't stop there, of course. Let's say you've got the gourmet coffee. So what, you're going to pour just plain old milk in it? Au contraire! You'll need eight types of sugars, flavored creamers, napkins with your corporate logo and gold-embossed little stirrers. You'll need a perky coffee guy in a freshly laundered white jumpsuit to appear every week to do cleaning, maintenance and deliver more gourmet brands to your excited staff. You'll have to hire a plumber to attach a line directly into the machine so that your water supply can be intravenously fed to make that perfect cup. Mmm, now that's good coffee!

And expensive too. This coffee service costs my client $100 to $150 per month. $100 to $150 per month!! For coffee. They only have 10 employees. And here's the crazy thing: half his employees come in to work holding steaming cups of coffee poured from old-fashioned pots at their local mini-mart or (gasp!) their homes.

What is with these gourmet coffee services? What business can afford to plunk down $150 per month on coffee? Have we gone insane?

Good business owners know this is nuts. They don't buy into this hype. Many are gracious enough to spring for a coffee maker and a can of Maxwell House from the local supermarket. From there the employees are on their own. Some people charge their employees for coffee. That's a little unfair. No one's saying you should deprive your employees of their coffee. For all we know the caffeine really does help people stay awake long enough to get your invoices out the door and your paperwork filed. Who's to argue with years of coffee drinking at the office?

But all this gourmet stuff is for the birds. There are ninety servings in a $4 can of coffee. If each of the ten people in a company drink three cups of coffee a day, that's only seven cans of Maxwell House a month, or $28. Compare that to the $150 per month coffee service and you're saving about $1,400 per year. Talk about a wake-up call!

Free Calling! Free Calling!

I've hit that stage of life when it's always me paying for stuff.

There used to be a time when people paid for me. My dad paid when we went out for dinner. My grandfather bought me gifts. My grandmother paid for baseball tickets. My employer reimbursed me for parking. People gave me checks when I got married. But that's all in the past now. Things have changed.

Now it's me who's picking up the check at lunch all the time. I'm paying for shipping. I foot the bill for holiday parties. I'm writing the bonus checks. I'm doling out $20 bills to my kids for movies, snacks, alcohol. My taxes go to pay for things that have nothing to do with me: welfare in Atlanta, a bridge to nowhere in Alaska, funding for a summit in Ireland.

So over a year ago I decided to take action. No more being pushed around. It was time for me to take a stand and make others pony up when the bill came due. So where to start? I couldn't exactly change the tax code or the way the government spends my money very easily. I'd have a mutiny on my hands if I canceled the holiday party. And my kids just wouldn't be as much fun without the money to get into trouble with. But I had to do something.

Then God spoke to me while I was driving down the turnpike. Here's what he said. "Conference Calls." That's right, conference calls. Must've been a slow day in heaven.

I looked at the books and found that my company was

actually spending about $150 a month on conference calls. Because we sell business software we do a lot of online demos and training. We also have project meetings with clients on the phone, too. The service we had been using since the time of Alexander Graham Bell was charging us a whopping 10 cents per minute per caller. It doesn't take much to spend 1,500 combined minutes. That's only 25 hours.

I made some changes.

I got rid of our conference-call service and started using one of those free online services. I'm not into naming specific products or services here, so just search "free conference call" and you'll find a bunch.

Guess what? This works. The service I chose allows unlimited (no joke here) calls with up to 100 people on a call. Each call can last up to six hours. It even records the calls for playback. And... it's free.

Not exactly free, but pretty close. Once you sign up on the website (no credit card needed) you get assigned a unique conference code and a regular phone number to call. Mine starts with 712, which I'm told is in Idaho. I pay for my call only. Everyone else calls the same number and uses the conference code that I give them. They pay for their call. If their long distance plan allows unlimited calls or cheap U.S. rates then they're not even affected.

But man, I was affected. In one month my cost of conference calls disappeared. Suddenly, I'm using the service all the time. I'm conferencing with my kids. I'm conferencing with my employees. I'm still trying to set up a conference call with Jimmy Page and Robert Plant about their reunion tour, but those guys are tough to reach.

How do these guys offer something for nothing? Believe it or not, they get a commission for each call routed through certain lesser-used telephone exchanges. I kid you not. God bless America!

131

The most important thing for people to know is that this stuff works. I've been using it for over a year without any issues. The reception is clear. The price is right. It's kind of a no-brainer. With all this money I'm saving I can buy my kids whatever they want.

Don't Mess With The People You Love

Don't mess around with your suppliers. You're not fooling anyone.

My friend John likes to read those business self-help books. Like most entrepreneurs, he wants to improve his cash flow. Many of these books advise readers like John to stretch out payments to their suppliers in order to improve cash flow.

"Your suppliers are the most affordable banks around," one expert puffs. John tried this and guess what happened? He almost jeopardized some of the most important business relationships he had. At one point, a supplier threatened to cut off a critical raw material until John got current with his debts. Other suppliers assumed that John's business was tanking because he was suddenly extending payments to them -- so they tightened up their credit policies and held back shipments.

"Next time I need financing I'll go to a bank," he muttered.

C'mon! Your suppliers don't know what you're up to? Believe me, they're reading the same books as John! They don't have bills of their own to pay? They don't take notice when your bills are notoriously late? They're probably like you and me -- businesses struggling to grow. Playing games with money that you owe them doesn't do a whole lot towards strengthening your relationship. It only makes than annoyed. And if you're relying on these suppliers to get you product in time, you really don't want them annoyed, do you?

Many big companies, like Fedex, Peco Energy Co, and

Verizon know this. They don't play games. Try "financing your business" by paying your shipping, electric or phone bills late. You'll quickly find yourself getting slapped with fines, fees and maybe worse. These people don't play around. They provide a service and rightly expect to be paid for that service on time. They're not in the financing business either. If they were then you'd call them... a bank.

Smart business people pay their bills early. They have a system for getting payables recorded and accrued. Upcoming bills are scheduled for payment. This way cash flow is managed intelligently. None of this robbing Peter to pay Paul stuff. Cash comes in, cash goes out and on schedule. If the business is being run correctly then there should be enough left over to call itself profits.

Make a schedule and stick by it. Pick two days a month for bill paying. Many people like to use the 10th and 25th of each month as their bill paying days -- it spreads things out. Don't cut checks on any other day but these two days, unless it's an absolute emergency. Manage your cash flow around these two days. If you can, take an early pay discount. Keeping things on schedule like this will allow you to put your thumb on your company's cash flow and manage things intelligently.

Your suppliers will like you for this. They'll know you're reliable and pay on time. They'll deliver to you on time. They'll give you the benefit of the doubt if there's ever a problem. They'll trust you. They'll want to do more business with you. They'll recommend you to their friends. They'll arrange marriages between your children and theirs. It's amazing what actually doing what one promises to do (like paying bills on time) does to a business relationship. It's almost refreshing!

One other thing about paying bills on time: Pay them in full, too. Don't play games. Don't withhold an entire invoice just because there's a question on one little line item. Get these issues out of the way early. Don't make your suppliers chase you down. You still owe the money. Smart managers settle their debts efficiently and pay more attention to making their customers happy.

Beware Those Biz Consultants

Phase 1: The hook

"Hi, I'm Bob from Acme Consultants and we'd like to offer you a free, no-strings-attached visit to evaluate your business and give to you a written report of recommendations to help you improve profitability."

Sounds like an interesting proposal, doesn't it? Well, we know that if it sounds too good to be true...

Bob's not a consultant. He's a salesman. And the report that Bob is selling is only the tip of the iceberg. "Acme Consultants" is not a consulting firm. They're a factory that takes advantage of small business owners. The report they're peddling is the hook. The expensive project they're going to try and sell you is what they're really after.

I know of some business owners who didn't figure this out. They took Bob up on the free report and free recommendations. They invited him in. And they got in trouble. Here's what could happen to you.

Phase 2: The line

Bob, professionally dressed, arrives right on time. Over a cup of coffee he reviews his excellent résumé with you. Fortune 1000 experience, management supervision, the works. Bob now works for "Acme Consultants" because, as he says it, "I wanted to get out and give something back to the small business community." How touching. How noble.

Bob gets to work. He sniffs around your offices. He walks through the plant. He flirts with your receptionist. He carefully takes notes. He asks brilliant questions like "would you like to make more margin on your product?" or "is increasing your cash flow important to you?" Finally, Bob leaves, promising to come back shortly with his recommendations.

And of course he does. With a frown, Bob sits across from his prey (that's you) and says, "I'm concerned." He says he's uncovered many issues. He makes a few suggestions about "speeding up collections" and "cutting overhead." He smiles and assures you that his report will cover it all. That is, if all you want is a measly old report.

"I don't think just a report is going to fix these problems," Bob whispers to you confidentially. "You need some real help here. We can help."

How can you resist? The guy seems to really care. He seems to really know what he's talking about. And he's telling you that your business needs help. He gets it. What can you lose by having Bob return with his team so they can really help you make some big changes here?

Phase 3: The sinker

Two days later you've got Bob and three other guys invading your conference room. They're all sniffing around, drinking your coffee and flirting with your receptionist.

After two days, Bob and his team meet with you again. But this time they've got a big thick document. The document lists all the woes that your (and every other) small business has and lays out a series of steps for addressing those woes. All involving Bob and his consultants. This is not a report. It's a proposal for consulting work. About $100,000 of consulting work. Bob wants to get things going "right away, before things get worse." Along with the document, Bob hands you a $5,000 invoice for services already rendered.

Bob just earned five grand for printing out a boilerplate

proposal, replacing your company's name for the name of his last victim. Suddenly Bob has a scary little look in his eye, as he explains to you that your actions to date have constituted acceptance of the work so far. Then his look softens as he assures you that the rest of your "investment" will pay off many-fold for years to come.

This is a true story. There are consultants out there who are preying on business owners. I have names. I have details. Need a good consultant? Get a referral or visit the Institute of Management Consultants (www.imcusa.org). There are many people out there who can truly help you. But not Bob.

Happy New Year! Give Me My Money!

My friend Jake is not a fan of parties and parades. He doesn't like champagne and thinks Ryan Seacrest is overrated. So you would think he dreads the new year, right? Wrong. Jake loves celebrating the new year.

Jake runs an engineering services company. His secret of success?

"First, provide excellent strategic planning, project management and design work to large organizations around the world," Jake said to me. "And then make sure to celebrate the new year."

Jake doesn't mean our traditional December 31 new year. Or Rosh Hashanah. Or the Russian Orthodox new year. Jake's religion is money. This religion celebrates its new year four different times every 12 months.

Sure, that big day comes on December 31. But other "New Year Days" come on March 31, June 30 and September 30. That's when most of Jay's vendors and customers end their quarters, even their fiscal years.

Jake buys and sells to large companies. For years he's been a watcher of calendars. Their calendars.

Jake invested over $250,000 in an advanced CAD/CAM system last year for his firm. As he narrowed down the potential systems during his search Jake made sure to find out each vendor's fiscal year end. So when he finally decided on the right software, he knew when to strike.

The software he bought was quoted at over $300K. During his research Jake found out when the software company's fiscal year came to an end. It's a good thing too, because this company was sneaky. Their fiscal year end wasn't until January 31.

Jake chose the software and then … waited. He pleaded poverty. He blamed the economy. He said his alimony was killing him (Jake's still happily married after 18 years). He said he had a bad crack habit. He said he owed his bookie. Whatever. He didn't return calls. He watched the sales guy sweat, not wanting to lose his big commission. Jake knows all about sales guys. He knows that they're all compensated on how they do each quarter, not to mention the year. They're all about making their numbers.

Jake celebrated the real new year. The Jan. 31 new year. In midmonth, Jake announced that he may … and he stressed the word may … be ready to buy. He and his wife were back together. He just got out of rehab. He struck oil. Whatever.

Then it was party time. Jake found himself showered with offers of lower prices, free training, extra support, women and booze. All of this from a salesperson (and his manager) who suddenly saw this big deal resurrected and just in the nick of time! They weren't going to let this fish get away. Jake took full advantage. He made sure to get a new year's present that came in the form of a big price reduction.

Jake loves to celebrate new years when he's selling too. Many of his customers are large companies: They're generally bureaucratic, poorly run and mismanaged.

He always calls on his big customers during budget season, which is generally three to four months before their fiscal year end, when they're putting aside money for next year's engineering projects. Jake wants to make sure he's on the list. He asks what projects are coming up and suggests

140

others. "There's only one time when everyone's thinking about the next year," Jake says. "So you've got to strike then."

Jake also tries to grab some more of this year's dollars too. He discovered a dirty little secret about large companies. Many of them are like the government. They prefer to spend money over saving it.

If there's money left over in the budget at the end of the year ... managers are desperate to get rid of it. Ask any good vice president at LargeBigCoUSA Inc.

"We must NOT show a significantly under budgeted line item on our departmental P&L this year. My God, how could we be under budget? Don't you realize we could lose the money we put aside for next year if we spend too little this year?" Fellow business people, I am not kidding.

So they spend it. On anything. Jake likes to be there with his hand out, suggesting small, yet overpriced engineering projects.

A true profiteer, Jake's real love of the new year comes from the time to squeeze a few bucks from both his vendors and his customers.

Don't Waste Money On A Fancy Office You Don't Need

This is a tale of two cities.

Mark is from San Diego and his company was in the business software industry. Knowledgeable, smart and conscientious, he's a very nice guy who did good work. Mark rented office space in a great place near the Gaslamp Quarter. He figured that clients would be impressed by his high-tech quarters. He added a training room and a state of the art conference facility. Two years later his business went under. He was the victim of a horrible fate shared by other businesspeople: Death By Rent.

I know another guy who distributes car parts out of a rat-hole in North Philadelphia. Not that he loves the location or anything, but he inherited the business from his father who had taken it over from his father a generation before when the neighborhood was somewhat respectable. Now he couldn't get very much for the place, so he stays there. There he is, hunkered down in a dilapidated building, graffiti on the outside, chewed up carpets and creaky steps on the inside. But he owns the place. And every day (before it gets too dark) he jumps into his BMW and drives back to his oasis in the suburbs.

Smart business owners understand that rent kills. Big offices are for big firms. Plush waiting rooms may impress your customers but low prices and quality products will keep them coming back (and keep you in business).

My company has grown significantly in the past 12

years. We've added hundreds of clients and almost a dozen people. Our "office" is a post office box in a Mailboxes Etc. Everyone works from home, or (better yet) at clients' offices. We're connected through the Internet. We share data on one of three computers that's stuck in the back of my basement. Our primary internal communication is e-mail and instant messaging. Our phone system, hosted by a company 3,000 miles away, forwards all calls directly to our cell phones.

We've never lost any business because we don't have an office. And we sure have saved a lot in rent.

A large office has an insatiable appetite for eating away at your profits. It will need to be lighted and heated and air conditioned. Remodeling, repairs and maintenance costs will be an ongoing commitment. Your lease agreement may be subject to annual renewals, made at the whim of the landlord. And speaking of the landlord, you may be subject to termination, removal and other hindrances on your business because, let's face it, he owns the building and you do not.

A lot of times I see clients with large offices where at least a third is underutilized or not used at all. Boxes of junk are stored in one room. Offices that were once intended for an expanding group are vacant. Great swaths of square footage on the shop floor remain open, begging for attention (or at least a game of indoor hockey).

Like a kid at the dessert table whose eyes are bigger than his stomach, the proud business owner dreams of a growing company that will one day fill all the extra space he's leasing, only to find himself buried in added overhead caused by his excessive rent costs. An ego does not need a desk and chair.

If you're in retail, or professional services, or manufacturing, you're going to need space to do your business. Just don't overdo it. I understand that some law firms need to have a prestigious address and some retail shops need to be located in a good spot at the mall.

But if you can manage to move into the low rent district, then go there. Keep the space at a minimum. Don't create unnecessary overhead. Be a penny pincher with your square footage. Use every inch to its max. Lease more only if you are completely sure that the added expense is going to serve to create more revenues, or greater productivity.

Feel Good... Get Audited

Did you give much to charity last year? I mean really, really give? Wouldn't you like to give a little extra? Contribute more to society? Feel better about yourself? Or at least impress your friends and family with your largess?

Well, tell you what -- next year I'm going to help you give a few thousand dollars more to your favorite charity. You too can be an upstanding and worthwhile human being. And best of all it won't cost you a penny.

All you need to do is get audited. That's right. Get audited.

No, I'm not talking about the Internal Revenue Service. I'm not talking about hiring some starched shirt morticians from a large accounting firm either. What you need is one of those hungry, greedy, selfish wolves who'll take your side and get back what you overspent with those evil, immoral and wicked corporate giants.

You need a real auditor. One with teeth. And on your team.

I can recommend a few names, but that's not the point. Go to Google and use these keywords combined with "audit": utility, telecommunications and freight. Now you're talking! Hey Exelon, Verizon, UPS ... your days are numbered. Here come the wolves!

There's a bunch of service firms out there who love to audit other service firms, especially the big and arrogant ones.

And most do it for free. Well, not exactly for free. Their deal is they take a cut ("just a taste, my good friend") of any savings they reap for your firm. If they don't find any savings, you don't pay a penny. A crazy concept from the good old days of business ethics: someone who gets paid only when he or she gets results. Imagine that!

You'll have to do a little legwork too. They'll need copies of your utility, freight or telecommunications bills back through time. They'll be asking questions. They'll drink a lot of your coffee and will threaten your women and children, too. But that's a small price to pay for hiring these animals to get back your money.

Some of those big energy, freight and telecommunication firms like to offer free "audit" services. Exelon will send in "energy auditors" to offer "advice" on "saving energy." Some insurance companies do the same. Oh sure, and I'm really going to start regrowing the hair on my head, too. These services are merely hollow recommendations to save on "future" costs. No one's going to give you any cash back once you've spent it. You'll need to bring in the real wolves to help you do that.

The audit wolves will go back as many years as they can. They will have their own software. Your data will be analyzed for wrongly billed taxes and tariffs, overbilled time, inconsistent rates, noncompliance with your contract and wrong surcharges. They'll assist in negotiating any money back and fixing contractual issues going forward. Of course, they'll also offer other consulting services for additional fees, but that'll be up to you.

The whole process takes a few months. If you spend $5,000 on these costs each month, then even getting back 3 percent from the past three years would put $5,400 in your pocket. Even after fees, you'd be up a few grand.

Now take that money ... and give it back! Make a contribution to a charity of your choice. Be that kind of corporate citizen you always wanted to be! Look yourself proudly in the mirror and say "I'm some kind of great person, aren't I?" And you are. You really, really are. Until the charity asks you for more money next year and you say no. Well, we're only as good as the last thing we do, right?

Get Out Of The Office

Here's an idea: get out of the office.

That's what Rob Bernstein does. Except he doesn't do it alone. He brings along his key managers too. Once a month they leave the office and travel all the way ... to a Hampton Inn about three miles down the road.

For a morning each month he sits there, shivering in an overly air-conditioned meeting room and talks about the business. With the people that are helping run the business. "It's the most productive four hours of the month," Rob told me. "And I really get a chance to catch up with the latest in hotel Muzak too!."

The whole morning, including the room, costs him about $300. But the return on investment is huge.

There are no phones. No one's poking their head in asking for "just a minute." There are no overlapping meetings. There are no pictures of horsey-faced kids playing soccer or sunburnt bald guys from the last corporate golf outing. It's just a plain old room where there's nothing better to do than talk about ... the company.

Some people like to get into the numbers at these meetings. But not Rob. He's into gossip. He wants to talk to his production manager about what jobs are causing problems and what people are creating bottlenecks. He needs reminders from his office manager as to what each person in the office actually does all day. He asks his sales manager about the customers she's speaking to. Are they happy? Any ideas for new products or services? Rob finds that going off-site opens people up. It makes them more comfortable to talk.

A good manager like Rob knows how to get maximum productivity out of these off-site meetings.

He keeps them short. "No longer than a morning." He hates those "corporate retreats" that last for days and cost a fortune. No one wants to be there. They want to be with their families. And besides, a typical business owner like Rob has the attention span of a 5 year old. Three or four hours is about all he can take, let alone his employees. I can relate to that.

He switches up the attendees. Different people are invited each time. Some managers don't always get invited. His employees love to get a chance to leave the plant for a morning, drink coffee and hobnob with the execs. Fresh faces bring fresh ideas. It's no fun to look at the same tired mugs each month. And management, knowing how the gossip flows at the Hampton Inn, gets nervous when they're not attending too.

He has a specific agenda for each meeting. Everyone knows what's going to be discussed in advance. There are no surprises. People have time to prepare. This isn't some exercise to catch someone off guard. It's not a game show. Rob needs information and answers to questions. It's only fair that people can prepare beforehand.

Once a perky employee jumped to her feet and enthusiastically suggested that everyone agree on a list of "action items." Bob fired her on the spot for being so annoying (ok, he didn't. But he really wanted to). Bob does keep notes. He assigns follow-ups to people. He sends a written document to everyone so they know who's responsible. Then he starts with the last meeting's list at the next meeting. Everyone's held accountable. Duh.

Are all your meetings in the office? Try something

different. Get out. Smart business owners and managers know the value of a change of scenery. Try taking a deep breath, stepping back, and making sure the boat's headed in the right direction. Rob's approach is to do this at the Hampton Inn once a month. It ain't the Four Seasons … but it's a whole lot better than his office.

Mike's A Mess, But His Warehouse Is A Thing Of Beauty

The fact that Michael usually doesn't shower over most weekends isn't really important. The fact that the backseat of Michael's '01 Camry still has left over food since '01 isn't important. The fact that Michael hasn't bought a new shirt for himself for over five years isn't important either. People are one way at home, and another way at work. And this business owner's no different.

It's because these things aren't so important to Mike. He likes how he smells. He's not bothered by the state of his car. He doesn't need new shirts. This is ironic. Ironic because if you visited Michael's place of business, where he distributes parts used for three major lines of farm equipment, you'd notice something really unusual. No, his own office is a complete pigsty. But it's his warehouse. That place is neat as a pin. Organized, efficient and clean.

Michael may not be a big believer in personal hygiene. But he's a major believer in warehouse efficiency. "I don't care what we're selling; the more organized our warehouse is, the more money we'll make," he says to his employees.

"Hey, Mike," one employee once jokingly said. "How about plowing some of those profits into a new wardrobe for yourself?" Poor guy's been out of work since that comment.

A key to Michael's warehouse management: his vendors. "I put a lot of pressure on them to help me stay organized," he said.

Mike's business seems simple, but it's not. He carries

thousands of parts for three main manufacturers of popular farm equipment. When someone needs a spare or replacement item they call him and he ships it out. His business survives on availability and the ability to get stuff out the door quickly. His major customers have repeat orders and special requests. His warehouse has 10 employees, and they're constantly running around. Lost time finding, packing and shipping stuff means lost money. Many business owners who carry inventory suffer the same challenges.

As does Mike. But he suffers them differently. He suffers them along with his suppliers. In tough times, suppliers will go to extreme lengths to make their good customers, like Mike, happy. Even if he wears the same shirt to work every day.

For example, Mike's big on scheduling. He keeps a window open for deliveries and works with his suppliers, and their carriers, to only make deliveries during that time. This way his people aren't being interrupted throughout the day as stuff arrives at the warehouse. He's had to be tough about this, even refusing to accept deliveries that arrived outside of an agreed time. But now he's got a system down. And his suppliers, having learned the system, can better plan their shipments.

You'd think because Michael's office is such a mess he wouldn't like to have people around. But it's the opposite.

"I love having my suppliers visit," he said. In fact, he has them come by regularly, at least every quarter. There are ups and downs to this approach. The downside to this is that his suppliers get to really look over the products that he has — both from them and their competitors. Some people might justifiably feel uncomfortable having outsiders take such a close look at their inventory.

But to Mike, there's a bigger upside. His suppliers advise him better ways to store their products. They give him hints of products to come. And they buy stuff back. Frequently, Mike winds up doing deals with them to buy back slow-moving products. Usually this is at a deep discount. But the loss is still less than carrying dead stock. Michael's relationship with his suppliers has improved because of this.

Mike's big into bar coding. He makes his suppliers big into it too. His rule is that every item that comes in the door has to be pre-bar coded. That saves him time. Each item is scanned into his inventory system. He's talking more and more about implementing an RFID (Radio Frequency Identification) system, too — and this will also involve a coordinated effort with his vendors. Mike's not the kind of guy who will do stuff like this alone.

Mike's in the business of inventory. But that doesn't mean he has to store everything himself. He's big into maximizing every square inch of his warehouse. He loathes renting more space. So he turns back to his suppliers and pushes them to keep as much inventory as they can. He's cut deals to pay them a warehousing charge if they store parts on his behalf — and then he can take the charge as a credit on future purchases if made within an agreed timeline. This works out for both parties — the suppliers get a confirmed sale and Mike gets them to take on the warehousing.

And when the items do come in the door, Mike's worked out how they're palletized too. Instead of just recciving a truckload of stuff, he's arranged in advance how the items are to be organized. This way his warehouse guys don't have to waste time re-sorting the products. They can pull pallets off the truck and take them directly to the right place in his warehouse. Some of the pallets may have already been designated for specific customers and Mike has worked out those technicalities in advance with his suppliers too.

Finally, Mike has a supplier manual. There's general information and vendor-specific information. He has all of the rules and procedures in the manual. He has specific terms, conditions and policies that he's agreed on with suppliers. It's shared with each supplier and updated frequently. That way if there's a dispute, they can go back to the manuals to find an answer.

Not bad for a disorganized, disheveled mess of a guy. It's amazing how some of us can be a complete mess in our personal lives, and yet successful in our professional lives. Just ask Mike. When it comes down to making money, smart business people find ways to adapt.

The Best Travel Deal Out There

In 1999 I made a lot of wrong predictions. I predicted that most computer systems would fail at the end of the year. I predicted that Madonna would grow old gracefully. I predicted that the Dow Jones industrial average, which closed above 11,000 in May of that year, would rise to over 20,000 over the next five years.

I was never very good with predictions.

I was also wrong about Tracey. She's a travel agent. And a really good one. I first met her in 1999, the year that the online travel website Expedia.com was spun off from Microsoft. At the time she worked in one of those travel agency chains with outlets in malls. As the Web grew in popularity back in the '90s and sites like Expedia and Travelocity came on the scene, I thought that was it for poor Tracey. She'd be out of the travel business and looking for something with better, longer-term prospects. Like an Internet company or a savings and loan.

But Tracey was no dummy. Sure, her fashion taste was limited to Reebok pumps and cargo pants. She liked Cher. She watched "Dawson's Creek." But she was better at predicting things than I was. Her professional sense was a lot more accurate. She knew something I didn't: People are too busy to do everything themselves. Especially cost-conscious business owners.

She was right. Tracey stayed in the travel business.

She's done well. The travel agency she worked for grew in popularity, despite the online services that came about around her.

How is this possible? Aren't there good travel related websites for business owners? Sure.

For example, TripAdvisor.com and Igougo.com are great sites to find out people's reviews of hotels and destinations. To get cheap airfares, people like to go to Travelocity.com, Airfarewatchdog.com and Bookingbuddy.com. To get good rates on rooms, others go to Dealbase.com, Hotwire.com and Priceline.com. Other sites like Kayak.com and Farecast.com bring this stuff together and compare rates from all over.

So with all these great sites available, it seems like the best thing a smart manager can do is go online to get the best deals, right? Wrong. Because when people ask me the best way to save money on travel I always say the same thing: Call Tracey.

Life has become more complicated. We can't be experts in everything. It's not just about money. It's about time and money. Both have huge value. And smart managers understand this.

They understand that travel agents really know what they're doing. And we, for the most part, don't. We don't know the routes that well. We don't know the system. We're not travel professionals. We run businesses. We make sure shipments get out the door. We complain about the economy. When it comes time to look for the best airfare or a great deal on a hotel room we're not familiar enough with the industry to know where to go. Travel agents do this for a living. We lean on them for advice.

We've tried all the travel websites. Their prices are pretty much the same. Tracey's prices are pretty much the same, too. I don't see travel agents coming up with that many better bargains than Expedia, but I don't see a lot of difference either.

So why are we fussing with it at all? Why not let Tracey do it?

We have better things to do. Travel agents take care of the paperwork. They do the hunting for us. They come back with options. They do the administrative and grunt work. We spend our time doing what we do. If the costs are generally the same, why are we wasting valuable time doing something that someone else can do for us? We get it.

I still like to make my predictions. I predict that Republicans and Democrats will one day work together in harmony for the good of the country. I predict that my hair will start growing back. I like the Washington Wizards to take the NBA crown next year.

OK, maybe those predictions won't come true. But here's one thing that will: travel agents like Tracey will always be a better option for business people like me looking to save time and get good deals on travel for their companies.

How To Avoid Disaster

I've suffered through a string of disasters over the past year.

MTV announced it was ending Jersey Shore. My softball team is having another winless season. The local Vinny T's shut down. My sixteen year old son just got his learner's permit. And of course...Battleship: The Movie. 2012's been tough. Very tough.

As bad as this year's been for me, I'm not getting a lot of sympathy from Mondale Smith. He's a Loss Control Manager for American Family Insurance, an 80 year old provider of commercial and personal insurance coverage. Mondale's job is dealing with his customers' disasters.

I'm told by Mondale that a few other people have been dealing with disasters of their own. In the last few years there were devastating earthquakes in Japan, Haiti, Chile, and China. There have been strong tornados tearing up homes and businesses in the Midwest. And torrential floods elsewhere. Look, I don't want to appear unsympathetic, but listen people: Jersey Shore was cancelled. Do you really think that kind of tragedy compares to a few drops of water and a little shaking of the ground?

Of course I'm just kidding. Jersey Shore wasn't that great a show anyway. And the natural disasters so many have people have lived through are terrible.

I spoke to Mondale recently. He's never watched Jersey

Shore and he had no help to offer me or my softball team. That's because when two of your ten players routinely strike out in slow pitch softball there's little that anyone can do to control that kind of disaster. But Mondale did have some thoughts on how business owners like myself can protect themselves if a disaster were to befall them. "For starters," he told me. "Check out your competition. Or your neighbor."

Mondale says that smart businesspeople are always making sure they're keeping up with the other guy. If you're operating a gift shop down the Jersey Shore, you're probably raking in the dough selling those Snooki T-Shirts. But what kind of business interruption insurance do you have if the weather turns south (or Snooki loses her 15 minutes of fame)? More importantly, what kind of business interruption policy does the guy next door have? If you're running a landscaping firm in Phoenix, what does your competitor on the other side of town do to make sure he's covered in case of a natural disaster? Different regions are subject to different kinds of disasters. A coastal business has to worry about flooding and (now we know) oil spills. A business that relies on tourists has to think about weather and terrorism. That bakery near Oprah's house in Chicago has to seriously worry when she decides to move to the West Coast.

Disaster insurance is nothing new. And neither is running a small business. Mondale tells his customers to talk to their competitors at trade shows or reach out to their industry groups. He suggests they consult their local chamber of commerce, query other insurance agents and cold call people in the same line of business to find out what kind of coverage they carry in case of a disaster.

Although American Family has a long record of paying out claims when they occur they're in the business to make money. Insurance companies like theirs would rather not pay anything out if they can avoid it. To that end, Mondale advises his clients to consider insurance as the very last resort.

"Insurance is not a profit exercise," he says. "It's there as a safety blanket if everything else fails."

So he tells his clients to always think ahead of what disasters could befall them and what they would do about it if bad things happened. Do they have a generator for alternate electricity? If they're in the restaurant business do they have a backup gas line? Is there another source of supply if a key vendor goes down? Do they Tivo "Glee"on BOTH the upstairs and downstairs TVs in case one of the Tivos doesn't record the right channel like it's &%$## supposed to? These disasters must be thought through in advance and a plan should be in place to address them. Before the insurance kicks in.

Separate your business assets too, Mondale tells me. Have a safety deposit box in another secure location for important documents and valuables. Backup your company data offsite or use inexpensive online services like Mozy. com or Carbonite.com. Ship your financial documents, like invoices and cancelled checks to a storage facility far away. Hide that bag of weed left over from that final Grateful Dead tour in the back of your closet so your kids don't find it. Don't worry – it'll keep until that night when they're all sleeping at Grandmom's.

And a good insurance agent will help too. Mondale's title is "Loss Control Manager." He doesn't like it when his customers lose money any more than they do. His agents are encouraged to proactively meet with their customers, walk around their facilities, interview their people, look at their financial operations and drink their coffee. They make recommendations for diversifying inventory, improving infrastructure and protecting their businesses against harsh weather. They look at the coverages and suggest the right amount, not the most they can sell. This is what good insurance agents do. Does this sound like your guy? As I'm writing this it definitely doesn't sound like my guy…except for the coffee part. Excuse me while I make a few calls.

160

Should a business owner carry a high deductible or a low deductible? Of course it depends on the company, but Mondale tells me he sees many of his clients carrying the higher option. It reduces the premiums they have to pay and puts more responsibility on them to cover the first chunk of damages they may incur. "I always tell these customers to just make sure they've got enough in the bank to cover this deductible if something really bad happens," he tells me. Carrying a higher deductible is definitely a risk. Not as risky as spending a weekend in Aspen with Charlie Sheen. But you're taking a chance. Most executives do. Just make sure you've got reserves somewhere.

Is there an upside to the disasters that have affected so many people this year? Mondale believes there is. "Those companies that were prepared will ultimately survive," he says. "And those that weren't...won't." To the victor remains the spoils. Business owners who don't think ahead wind up going out of business. And who grabs their customers? Smart businesspeople who plan ahead and prepare for when bad things happen. These are the people that ride out the storm and expand their business when the worst is over. That's because things always come back. Don't believe me? Just ask Betty White.

Jessica's Smart Boyfriend

Jessica Taylor has been dating the same guy for almost two years. They're very close. Not only do they live together but they're also business partners. They own a small real estate brokerage firm in the city.

Jessica's boyfriend is kind and considerate. But, like many guys, he's afraid to make a commitment. In the two years she's known him she's never heard him say to her those three magic words.

Recently that changed. Jessica's boyfriend discovered something about himself and Jessica. He realized what was missing from their relationship. And so, one late afternoon, at the height of the couple's passion, her boyfriend grabbed hold of Jessica, tipped her chin so that she could look directly into his eyes and, after taking a deep breath, finally uttered those three magic words. Not exactly the words she expected to hear. But better.

"Sprang Eco Sans." He whispered to her. "Sprang Eco Sans."

Now, these words may not stir up emotions for most females. But for those females that are also penny pinching business owners, no three words could be sweeter.

Sprang Eco Sans is a font that Jessica's boyfriend discovered on the internet. It's for real. And it's free.

He googled it. He downloaded it. He quickly installed it on every computer in their office. The font, invented by researchers in the Netherlands, is unique. It has tiny little bitty circles that are unnoticeable to the human eye when letters are printed. But because of these little bitty circles, a printer uses less ink. Anywhere from 30-40% less ink. And that means less replaceable ink cartridges too.

Ahhh. Sprang Eco Sans. Those three beautiful words.

Jessica's a romantic at heart. She loves getting flowers and going out to candlelight dinners with her boyfriend. She cries at those stupid romantic comedies with Hugh Grant. She still believes that Jon and Kate will one day get back together and re-discover their love.

But Jessica's also a penny pinching business owner. And, like the rest of us, she feels like she's selling her soul to Satan every time she buys another damn $15 ink jet cartridge for the $99 printer she purchased at Staples. Every time, by the way, means just about every week. She knows that the printer companies that charge for these ink jet cartridges are evil. She knows that she's getting about a dollar's worth of ink for every $15 cartridge she's buying. And it bothers her like nothing else.

So when Jessica's boyfriend uttered those three magic words, Sprang Eco Sans, it was poetry to her ears.

She can wait a few more months until he says those other three words. She's a penny pincher. For now, she's happier with these three.

But Jessica's boyfriend wasn't done. This guy really knows how to get to her heart. That's because he discovered yet ANOTHER way to reduce the amount of ink their business was using and hence to lower the costs of those dreaded ink jet cartridges. He discovered a software application called InkGard.

InkGard (www.inkgard.com) takes ink conservation to another level. It's only $10 to buy or free if you purchase a few printer cartridges from the company. The software gets installed on each workstation.

It's easy to download and simple to install. In fact, it installs itself as another printer on your Windows machine. So what's so special about InkGard?

Jessica set it as her "default printer" for each computer. That way whenever she's printing out a document an InkGard screen comes up first, asking her to set her desired "SmartInk Control Savings".

It's a big dial. And a big deal. If she's printing out an important proposal she uses a 30% savings. If she's printing a photo of her (now cherished) boyfriend she cranks down the ink savings to 0%. But most of the letters, documents and other output goes through at a 50% savings.

Depending on the savings she chooses, the documents come out that much lighter-looking. But still very, very readable and very, very useable. With much, much less ink. Default savings can be set so everyone in the company is using the same each time. There's even a tool that lets her track her historical ink usage. Since putting in InkGard Jessica is estimating she's cut down this ink useage by another 25%. And let's just say her boyfriend, the guy who came up with this idea, is reaping a few rewards elsewhere. Eh, guys? Eh?

But was Jessica's boyfriend through? Oh no. He was on to a good thing.

He went around to each printer and made sure that its default setting is to print "draft" quality documents. Jessica knows that she can change the quality to a better setting if printing out something that's going to a customer. He also downloaded a free PDF creator software from PrimoPDF (www.primopdf.com) so that Jessica, rather than printing and mailing documents, could just create PDFs of her invoices, orders, quotes and purchase orders and email them. This significantly cut down on the amount of printer ink Jessica was using.

And how about those new printers that we're seeing advertised? The ones that promise to use much less ink? Jessica's boyfriend hasn't fully investigated those yet. But it's on his list of things to do for her. Ahead of getting her flowers or candies. She doesn't mind.

That's because this guy knows the way to his girl's heart. She's not a typical girl, this Jessica. She's a penny pinching business owner. Flowers and candies may be OK for some. But saving her lots of money on printer ink? Why, that's enough to win her over for life.

Blame Microsoft

I was in a Rite Aid the other day and about to pay for my stuff at their new bank of automated check out kiosks. I heard one woman behind me say to her friend, "Oh, I would NEVER use those things. They take away jobs from people." Um...duh?

What's that? You'd like to work for my small business? I appreciate your interest. And I, like so many others, feel terrible about how long you've been unemployed. We would like to do something about the situation. We'd like to help you. But there's something you (and the woman from the Rite Aid) need to know. I'm not sure how to say this kindly so it's best I just say it: many of us don't really need more employees.

Of course the fact that you're out of a job has a lot to do with the state of the economy. Growth is anemic. The uncertainty in the current business environment is holding a lot of us back from making the investments that we'd like to make. And regulations and the prospect of more regulations, let alone higher taxes to pay for our country's deficits, are giving many of us pause for concern. For that we can certainly blame many: our politicians, the government, the banking system, the media...even ourselves.

But it's not just that. In fact, a good reason why you don't have a job and your prospects of finding a job are not encouraging can also be blamed on someone else. Microsoft.

And other technology companies like them.

Because there's something else going on in this economy. Our country's Gross Domestic Product, while growing at a painfully slow pace, is now higher than it was before the 2008 recession. And yet it's common knowledge among those who track these things that there are more than seven million people without jobs than there were at the same time. Which means that businesses are producing more products and services than ever before...but with seven million less people.

Manufacturers are leading the charge. Just look at how manufacturing productivity has risen over the past thirty years in this country while the number of people employed to make stuff has decreased.

I know you need a job and I know this is a very difficult situation. And I don't want to sound cruel because I'm trying to help you. And to get help with a problem the first thing we have to do is diagnose the problem. So here's the cold, hard truth about why you're unemployed: most businesses don't need you any more. We can do just as much, if not more, without you.

Over the past twenty years, the technology industry, led by companies like Microsoft, have given us powerful databases, operating systems, networks and software applications that have made it easier for us to accomplish more tasks that we did before with less people. And it's not just Microsoft who you can blame.

Blame Sage, who makes Enterprise Resource Planning and Customer Relationship Management software that has enabled businesses to automate their marketing campaigns, build workflows for alerting managers when inventory needs to be replenished and generate workorders and invoices that are immediately emailed without employing teams of people.

Blame Rackspace and Amazon and other cloud based infrastructure providers, who allow us to host all of our business applications on their servers, thereby eliminating many in our information technology departments and cutting back on wasted time from downed computers and security flaws.

It's true that the costs of healthcare and other regulations have discouraged many of us from hiring full time employees. But at the same time we've come to realize that maybe we don't need as many full time employees as we used to. And because technology has advanced so much, even over the past few years, we've seen an explosion of outsourcing among businesses, both small and large.

For little cost, companies like mine can easily setup systems for remote access and collaboration. We use services again from Microsoft , but also from companies like Citrix Online and LogMeIn so that remote people can access our networks to do their work. We use cloud based applications like Box.net, Basecamp, Salesforce.com and NetSuite to share documents, files and data with both employees and contractors wherever they are. Thanks to Microsoft, Google and companies like Zoho and Dropbox we can now easily put out entire office in the cloud – documents, spreadsheets, presentations, databases, projects.

And we can communicate with our outsourced help, wherever they are, more quicker and easier than before. We make free phone calls using Skype and inexpensive mass calls (or texts) using products like VoiceShot. We hold free conference call sessions using Freeconferencecall.com. We share our desktops using Glance and Join.me. We hold training sessions using Webex. We use video tools like Oovoo to virtually meet face to face.

And finding outsourced help is easier than it's ever been. That's because we can search sites like Craigslist, Elance and Guru. And when we find qualified people to accomplish specific tasks for us we can use the sites to set our relationships, manage our payments and communicate our needs.

Which is why so many of the tasks once done by companies are now being outsourced to individuals and other companies who can, using their own internal technology, perform these same tasks with so many less people. Most of the clients I work with outsource their payroll to companies like ADP and Paychex. Many outsource their bookkeeping needs to firms that do nothing else, but do it more efficiently. Most companies now have internet based phone systems where an automated attendant re-directs calls to people's cell phones and voice mail messages are sent to them via text with no humans in the middle.

No humans.

Are you starting to see the picture? I know you want to be hired full time by me. And I want to be doing my part. But please understand: I'm running a business. I want to make profits. And these tools are letting me make more profits by employing people only when I need them rather than carrying them on my payroll.

It's not all Microsoft's fault. What they're doing is nothing compared to what's happening on the shop floor. Because, quietly and without fanfare, companies like the Oystar Group are making machines that fill tubes faster than before, requiring less shifts of people to complete an order. And equipment from Keller Technology that creates more efficient machines so cosmetics and pharmaceutical manufacturers can produce more product with less people. And software and consulting firms like Intuitive ERP and Epicor who help manufacturers change their internal processes to create more products from less space and using less resources, particularly people.

We know this is true in our own lives. Things are lasting longer and working better. We're keeping our cars well beyond 100,000 miles. We're letting our fridges and toasters and kettles do their jobs well beyond the lifespan that our parents did. New developments in flooring, painting and construction are resulting in longer use of our homes. Because technology is better. Have you ever had a TV repairman to your house? How many times has your washing machine broken down over the past twelve years and thousands upon thousands of cycles? Because of technology, there are less people needed to manufacture and service the durable equipment that we use because this stuff is working better and for a much longer period of time.

And with all that, we still need you. Don't believe me? Look at things like the Monster Employment Index or read Gallup's Job Creation data analysis. Both surveys find that job availabilities are at their highest level than before 2008. But these are not same the jobs that existed before 2008. That's because we don't need as many receptionists, clerks, cashiers, bookkeepers, inventory stockers and maintenance people as we used to. Technology has helped us cut back on all of that. Go to your local supermarket (or Rite Aid) and you'll see what I mean.

But we do need programmers. And experienced customer service people. We need engineers, scientists, high end equipment operators, good service people and (very soon) capable construction workers too. In other words: people with skills. As a business owner it's a no-brainer to me that if I can profit from your skills I may very well be persuaded to hire you. What expertise can you bring to me that a machine can't do for much less? I have to meet that challenge with my own customers. That's the challenge that we all face.

Of course, all economies are cyclical. And more jobs will be created once the economy again begins to grow. No one knows when this will happen and right now, in our current political environment, many aren't feeling too confident that this will happen anytime soon. But even in a growing economy will we ever see 5-6% natural unemployment again? This may never happen. And if it doesn't, please don't just blame the politicians. Blame Microsoft. And other tech companies like them. Because it's because of them that I'm not hiring you.

I Run The World's Most Dysfunctional Company

I run the world's most dysfunctional company.

There are only ten of us. A few are proper employees and the rest of my people are made up of subcontractors. My company's grown since 1994 when it was only myself and my dad running it. My dad passed away a few years ago so now it's only me. We're not growing very fast but we're profitable. We have a good, stable client base and we all work hard.

But we're dysfunctional. That's because we're not really a company. We're a "virtual company." We have no offices. Sure, we're saving a ton of money and being very efficient this way. But building a a great team under this model is almost impossible.

There are a lot of us out there – virtual companies. My company provides technology consulting, which is a typical virtual company description. We specialize in sales and marketing technologies, particularly customer relationship management software. We sell, install, configure, customize, train and support. We integrate our software with other software products. So even though we don't do anything unusual our people are, by default, unusual. We are made up of tech people, database people, programmers and other such nerds. We come from as far away as the Ukraine and as close as New Jersey. We have our extroverts too – trainers and project managers. It's a combination of dysfunctional people, all brought together to do their tasks.

Except we're really not together. That's because we have no offices. We used to have offices, but I shut them down a long time ago. I decided to do this because every morning I would open up the doors, sit behind my desk and wait...for no one to come. All of our people would be out working at our clients. Or they would just work from home, because that was easier and because they wouldn't have to actually deal with other people face to face. Remember – these are techies. I sometimes go into other offices and wonder what that would be like. Getting coffee and asking someone if they had plans for the weekend or how their kid's doing at college.

We don't have that all. If you want to meet with me in my office you'd need to be treated with a shrink-ray so that you could fit into the post office box I maintain in a strip mall outside of Philadelphia. I used to fear that moment when an important client or partner would want to get together in my office and I would have to admit that I had no office. But that fear was unnecessary. When people want really want to meet I either suggest their offices or a local Starbucks. It works just fine.

So we're "virtual." Which means everyone works from their homes. To do this I rely on technology to keep us together.

For years I used to have a Windows Terminal Server in the basement of my house next to my cat's litter. I installed our main accounting and database applications on that server and whenever anyone needed information they would connect in and do their work remotely. This worked great until I realized that my cat was using the server as his own personal litter box. I won't get into the details of what a cat's urine can do to a Dell PowerEdge over a period over time, but let's just say the server went down. Permanently. So I got rid of it and now have all of my applications and databases hosted by an outside company. This costs a little more, but is still a better setup for us because it's faster, easier to access and for once someone is actually doing backups and implementing security properly. The cloud helps me run my dysfunctional company.

The cloud provides other tools to help me too. For example, our phone system is completely hosted. You'd never know when you call our toll free number. A friendly, but automated voice answers the phone and gives you the usual options of being transferred to sales, service or a dial by name directory. Everyone maintains their own voicemail boxes and gets calls forwarded to their home office lines or cell phones. Our email is, of course, hosted, so everyone can access their messages using whatever email application they like straight through their browsers. When more than one of us wants to talk about a client we use one of the many free conference calling services available. In the rare instances when we want to see who we're speaking with we Skype. We also use desktop sharing tools to demo software products or go over design changes. Our quotes, invoices and project plans are saved on the cloud. We use Google Apps, Microsoft Office's SkyDrive and DropBox. All of these tools helps to further our dysfunctionality.

But I can't blame technology for being so dysfunctional. Our people contribute very much to our eccentric corporate makeup. As mentioned before, the majority of the people in my company are subcontractors. They are local and also come from all over the world. You can find them all online nowadays through sites like Elance and Craigslist. I am extremely careful about being compliant with the IRS' subcontractor rules. So I limit the number of hours a subcontractor works each week. I require all the proper tax paperwork as well as a signed contractor agreement, complete with a non-compete clause (for which I'm pretty sure I could never enforce). I make sure that my subcontractors are themselves incorporated and do work for others and not just my company. I require that they invoice me each week and their invoices are treated no differently from our other vendors. Of course they are required to have their own office space as I can't provide one for them. I do give them a company business card, email address and voicemail box so they can conduct communications without confusing our clients. But they receive no other benefits, no vacation, no health insurance and no other compensation that would be perceived to be part of an employer relationship.

Amazingly, everyone seems to be happy with this arrangement. That's what you get when you hire oddballs, I guess. Most of the people who work for me have been doing so for many years. They enjoy running their own businesses and treating me like one of their clients. Because these are primarily technology people they are very independent. They are odd. They work odd hours. They frequently drink blood instead of coffee. They go for days without bathing. They send me emails at 3AM and are sometimes asleep at noon. A few still live with their parents, I think. I don't ask. They do this all without my close supervision. As long as they get the job done well and on time, I have no problem with the methodology.

Sure, it's a very, very profitable setup. I have almost no overheads. No rent. No utilities. No gourmet coffee machine rental. Almost all of my costs are variable. My employees get a salary, but other than a minimum of administrative hours I allow, my contractors only get paid when they're billable to my clients. I cover their out of pocket expenses for travel or supplies but I've learned a few good ways to bill these costs back to my clients (that's a topic for another time). Plus – we don't waste time. There's no chit-chatting in the hallways or talking about the latest episode of Mad Men at the coffee machine. When we speak to each other it's about work, work, work. Our calls are normally short and to the point. We don't spend a lot of time gossiping. That's because even after working together for so many years we really don't know each other that well. Can you believe that we only get together as a group once a year for a holiday lunch? And even then I never get full attendance – someone always seems to have something else going on or some aversion to social interaction that restricts them from attending.

Which is why my "virtual" company is so dysfunctional.

Because even though it may seem like people are wasting their time gossiping in the office, they're really not. They're building relationships. They're forming face to face, human bonds with each other. And this is useful when one person needs help from another. There's value in the chit chat. There's gold in the client gossip. Even though it sometimes may appear inconsequential, discussions in the office oftentimes lead to new insights about clients and new ideas about jobs. Things come out in casual conversations, like a new app tool or a cool website, that would never come up in one of our point-to-point conference calls. Information is exchanged and this information helps people do their jobs better. This is not happening in my company. Everyone is working in their own silo. I'm exchanging cost savings and some productivity for a loss in ideas, teamwork, relationships, creativity and innovation.

Maybe there's a way to improve this. But for now we'll continue to be profitable. And dysfunctional.

Managing Your Cash Flow

Over Time

Jessica Alba's Credit Crisis

I once read that a movie that Jessica Alba was making had been delayed because of what appears to be a lack of financing. Are you kidding me? This is Jessica Alba we're talking about! She is, like, so awesome! And now I'm told her movie can't get financing?

As a business owner, I am outraged. This sounds very similar to what I'm reading about fellow business owners around the country who also can't get financing. Of course the news about Jessica Alba is way more alarming. No argument there.

But what about the food manufacturer in Chicago that organized protests against its bank for pulling its financing? And the auto dealer in Atlanta who accused his bank of "fraud and misappropriation of funds" because that same bank forced him into bankruptcy after he defaulted on his loans? And what of that nice lady in Florida who can't get financing to open a preschool? And the couple in New Smyrna Beach, FL, who can't get the money to expand their golf club?

The government is accused of doing too little for small business. I'm hearing the Small Business Administration isn't guaranteeing enough loans. Meanwhile, the banks are accused of hoarding their cash to make their balance sheets look better. And companies that need cash are complaining that getting money is much harder than it ever used to be.

And now I hear that Jessica Alba's film also once ran into financing troubles? Damn you, Bear Stearns! This is all your fault!

Maybe all those small businesses and Jessica Alba really do have something in common. Maybe it's because they're finding out that it is harder to get financing than it was, say two or three years ago. Remember those days? That was when grizzly bears in the Bronx Zoo were getting loans to buy houses in White Plains, N.Y. When we were playing gin rummy with all the approved credit cards that kept arriving in the mail. When bankers rushed to back Jessica Alba classics like 'Good Luck Chuck' and 'The Love Guru'.

Sorry, Jessica. But those days are over.

But don't worry. You'll continue to be fine. And so will many business owners looking for funding. The system isn't completely frozen.

The fact of the matter is that most banks have plenty of money to lend to small businesses. They're just not lending the money like they used to. Instead, they're doing this crazy thing: lending only to those people who have the capability of paying the loan back.

"It was a big party for the last 10 years," says Robert Tabas, CEO of Royal Bank America in Narberth, PA. "But we're well funded and happy to loan to small businesses."

Royal Bank America, like many other community banks, received bailout money from the government. And yes, they used it to shore up their balance sheets. But banks make money when they lend money. That's what they do. They're just doing it a little differently right now.

"We always reviewed cash flow," says Tabas. "But now we're looking at more global factors, like the economy, the customer's industry, and their long-term plans."

Get used to it: Banks are just not giving out as many

loans as they did in the past. And they're making smarter, less riskier loans, too. They're giving more emphasis to credit reports. They're demanding tangible assets as collateral, not valuations from Cousin Vinny. They're leaning more towards established businesses and away from riskier startups. They're demanding detailed business plans and commitments by the business owner. They're going back to the basics. They're spending more time getting to know their customers, so they can get comfortable with their track record.

This is called due diligence. It wasn't being done by many lenders in the last 10 years. Banks and investors ran after those high-profit, complicated, mortgage-based-whatever deals. They lent money to people with sexy real estate projects like strip malls in Texas and condos on the Florida coast. They financed 'The Love Guru' for God's sake!

Smart business owners can see at least three benefits from tightened credit.

For one, the cream rises to the top. Like the producer who somehow got financing to make one of those ill-conceived Jessica Alba films, our competitors who were getting easy financing for their ill-conceived businesses are finding that the well has gone dry. As they become overwhelmed by their debt maintenance the truth comes out: They managed things poorly. Can anyone say General Motors? Every major bankruptcy we've seen has, at its core, a loan that couldn't be repaid. Maybe we can buy them out. Or they might choose bankruptcy. In any case, like Jessica's next film, they'll probably either suffer from lack of funds or completely disappear.

Second, bankers are now offering more reasonable financing. It may not be as much as we want. But it's probably as much as we can afford. It's based on what we're able to pay back, not on some unrealistic projections, but on the reality of today's business climate. Bankers are making more prudent business decisions and in the meantime doing us a favor. They're forgoing some of those way-too-profitable interest payments and fees in lieu of making a good investment for a reasonable payback. And we're not being sucked into a financing deal that we could never afford to pay back anyway.

Finally, banks are now way more involved in our businesses. No longer distracted by those crazy deals, their people are spending more time looking at our financial statements and business plans. They're making suggestions and offering assistance. These good people are MBAs and CPAs. These are experienced, prudent people who work with and help hundreds of small companies like ours. You know who they are: The kind of guys that don't have a prayer of ever dating Jessica Alba. But they do bring knowledge and insight to a business relationship. Previously we couldn't even get them on the phone. Now they're calling us to "check in," and even taking us out to lunch!

So this lack of financing is not as bad as some may think. And there's more good news: Jessica's film got back on track. "Thanks to the fans. I do movies for you. Practice safe sex and drive hybrids if you can," she is quoted on IMDB. We will, Jessica. God bless.

Why Are You Still Not Banking Online?

When it comes to helping entrepreneurs compete, I try to eat my own dog food. All the tips and strategies I share I aim to apply at my 10-person technology consultancy. But I have to come clean: I'm woefully negligent in one crucial area--and it's costing me.

I'm talking about online banking. Embarrassing as it sounds, I don't do it. Nor, as it turns out, do roughly 95% of my 500 clients. Why? Sheer laziness, I suppose.

Cindy Hom, on the other hand, is anything but lazy. She runs a 10-person fitness and wellness center in downtown San Francisco called Apex Wellness. She teaches people how to take care of their bodies, eat right and live fully through Pilates, Yoga and Martial Arts. And when it comes to banking, Cindy does it quicker and better than most because she bothered to figure out how to do everything online.

Here are some quick numbers for context. I pay my bookkeeper $20 an hour. She cuts maybe 100-150 checks a month for me. It takes her about five to six hours to enter the data, print it, stuff it and mail it. I probably spend another hour, worth $150 of my billable time, to review these checks. Then I pay another $100 a month for the cost of forms, postage and ink. All in, this process costs me about $400 a month. That's not chump change in any economic environment.

Cindy does what I do, but she gets it done for free. Her bank does it for her. Most big banks will.

When Cindy started her company a few years ago, she made a point of contacting all her vendors and preparing them for electronic payment. While plenty of small businesses haven't adopted online banking, large phone companies and utilities certainly have. All she had to do was hand over her vendors' bank names, routing codes and account numbers; from there, her bank sluices payments directly from her account to her vendors'.

Recurring expenses--like interest on a bank loan, car payments or rent--are paid automatically, and Cindy receives notification by e-mail. It all happens in a day, so vendors get their money quick, no matter where in the world they are. And she's not even losing the float: Cindy can schedule a payment up to the day before it needs to be made, rather than sending a check out days before and hoping it gets received on time.

But banking online isn't just about streamlining transactions. Cindy can also check balances and cash flow; print out reports; and receive e-mail reminders when bills are coming due. Her bank guarantees on-time payment, helping Cindy avoid late fees. The bank also stores all statements and check copies on its servers--no cluttered cabinets necessary.

Did all of this take some time to set up? Sure, maybe 15 hours. But that up-front investment has yielded big returns. "I'm saving lots and lots of time," says Cindy, munching on some granola. "I'm a trainer, not an accountant." Better yet, Cindy doesn't have a bookkeeper. She estimates that online banking is probably saving her about a day's worth of her time every month--allowing her to spend more time with clients and generate more cash.

Well done, Cindy. Heck, maybe you should be writing this book.

Your C.P.A. Is Not G.O.D.

Take it from me, a CPA: the only thing worse than a CPA is a CPA-GIHOM. That's a Certified Public Accountant who's also a Genius In His/Her Own Mind.

The CPA-GIHOM is the person who's just so much smarter than everyone (or so he thinks). His clients kowtow to him: "Oh, I need to run this decision by my CPA" or "My accountant would never allow this." He makes his clients feel that anything financial is his domain only. Only he can determine whether a decision is the right decision. Why do some business people lay down their swords in front of their esteemed CPAs, as if they're God?

Smart managers know that a CPA is not God. If he were so smart then how come he's got a bunch of small business clients like you and not advising the executives at General Motors? How come his office is located on top of a Chinese restaurant at the strip mall down the street? Why isn't he jetting off to vacations in the Maldives instead of that cabin his family owns near the lake?

Of course, there are some great CPAs out there. Like Bob Newhart, or the guy in the movie "Dave" who helped balance the nation's budget. That was really amazing.

And there are other professionals who provide solid business advice on top of the usual tax preparation work they do. Men and women who are trusted by their clients to give them sound opinions, based on their experiences with other clients in their industry. Like any profession there are good accountants and not so good accountants.

But we know that many CPAs are just... accountants. A small business CPA is most likely to be just expert in taxes. That's what they know and that's why you're buying their services. We know that just because a guy can fill out a tax return doesn't automatically make him a great business adviser. Or a genius either.

CPAs have all sorts of ways that they can take advantage of your fears. But you don't have to be a sucker.

For example. Ever read the Accountant's Report that's on the front of your financial statements?

Check it out... for a laugh. Basically, the accountant says "I take no responsibility for these numbers." Not exactly a hearty vote of confidence! Plus, by the time your accountant gets you the financials, hasn't hell frozen over? So why does your bank require it? Maybe because they don't. Maybe no one's even reading it!

A good manager will find out from his banker if just a tax return will suffice. There's a good chance the bank will waive the financial statement requirement and you can save on the extra fees your trusted CPA is charging you to prepare those irrelevant financials.

Here's another warning: avoid time and materials billing. CPAs are loathe to put a fixed price on their services. Everything's an estimate. This way they can blame us if things take longer than expected or bake in extra time for that new kid they hired who's trying to learn a debit from a credit.

My advice? Each year we should all sit down with our accountants and nail down a fixed price to do a task (like prepare an individual return). We should push to get it lowered. We shouldn't be afraid to extend our returns if it means it can be done during a slower period (like any good contractor, CPAs will lower fees for work done during their off-season).

And we shouldn't be afraid to split up the work either. Just because one CPA does our business return doesn't mean that another guy can't do our personal one. It's not a requirement. Besides negotiating an overall lower fee, we can have two CPAs offering their advice instead of one.

If you can stomach all those geniuses, that is.

Is Your Bookkeeper Stealing From You?

Bravado. Chutzpah. Guts.

These are the qualities I admire in people. And you know who I really admire? Bookkeepers who steal from their employers. They've got the biggest set of you-know-whats around. Their methods are obvious. They always seem to get caught in the end (remember, these are not brain surgeons).

What amazes me the most isn't the bravado of the corrupt bookkeeper, but the dopiness of the victim. Some business owners can be so blind and trusting.

"I thought the business was doing fine," said one sad little man, a business owner from Indianapolis. "Then all of the sudden I was facing bankruptcy."

"He looked like everybody's favorite uncle" said another dopey guy, describing the bookkeeper who had stolen hundreds of thousands of dollars from his company.

"She just seemed so trustworthy," lamented another gullible one.

Like I said ... dopes.

Don't believe me? Go and read some articles about employee theft and embezzlement. It's a case study in dopey business owners. These are people who take their eye off the ball and pretend that everything's going great. They ignore big warning signs. Yet these are the same business owners that yell and scream if a vendor overcharges them ten bucks.

Are you a dope? How will your bookkeeper steal from you? Good managers know. Dishonest bookkeepers steal in very obvious ways.

Some blatantly just write your company checks to themselves or people they owed money to, fake your signature, and hide the transaction from your eyes. Others create a bank account for a fake company and then write checks to that account as if they're a new supplier. Or another good one: opening up a bank account in the company's name (with the bookkeeper being the check signer) and then depositing customer checks there, available for future disbursements. When a business owner is in La-La land, the thieving bookkeeper can just take advances from American Express and then alter the bill. Or write out a few innocuous checks to cash ... and cash them.

Far-fetched? Science fiction? Nope. These are all actual examples from actual companies. Where were the business owners through all this? Out to lunch. In Disneyworld. Thinking of the next round of golf.

Smart managers don't fall victim to small-minded, uncreative little swindlers. They do some very basic stuff to prevent this.

Basic like having their accountant or some other outside party reconcile their bank accounts every month. Canceled checks go straight to the reconciler, not the bookkeeper. Signatures are examined. Differences are investigated.

Basic like requiring vacations. Force your bookkeeper to take a week or two off. Have someone else do his or her job. You may get a surprise or two.

Basic like keeping your checks locked up in your drawer. When a check run is needed have your bookkeeper give you a list of bills to be paid and then you can release just those checks required. Leaving blank checks lying around the office, or under the supervision of an employee, can be a temptation to someone with a gambling problem or, worse, an addiction

188

to Starbucks.

Basic like reading your general ledger. It's not exactly Tom Clancy, I know, but get a printout of your revenue and expense accounts and just make sure there's nothing goofy, like checks made out to your bookkeeper's veterinarian.

Basic like doing a simple employment check. It's amazing how many bookkeepers get to jump from job to job and steal money along the way because their employers are too busy (or lazy) to properly check them out.

Basic like getting out of the construction business. (I don't know what it is about bookkeepers, larceny, and the construction business, but there's way too much of a connection there.)

The Internal Revenue Service reaches into your pocket. The phone company lightens the size of your bank account. Your attorney gets his piece. But at least here you know where the money's going. Letting your bookkeeper walk out of your company with your money is definitely something only a dope would allow, not a smart business person.

Accounting Software Only Sounds Boring

Most business people I know think that accounting software is boring. Not as boring as say, sitting through the movie "Watchmen." Or waiting in line at Starbucks while some idiot discusses what flavor of tea he should choose (it's TEA for God's sake). Or listening to NPR.

But accounting software can be fun. Fun, I say!

Jason has lots of fun with his accounting application. He's the owner of a 20-person firm that distributes party supplies. His company's all about inventory. He's spent the time to make sure that inventory is tracked in great detail by his accounting software. This is not an easy task as he's got over 10,000 items. Oh, and a lot of helium for balloons. Now, that's fun.

Jason's completely obsessed with quarterly cycle counts, weekly spot counts and semi-annual physical counts. His warehouse is cleaner than my kitchen, but that's only because I have teenage kids who specialize in home destruction. Jason's inventory records are even cleaner than his warehouse floor.

A lot of business owners ignore inventory management in their accounting software. Some don't like keeping detailed records because they don't want to reveal too much to the tax guy. But using these features can keep this asset under control and therefore save lots of money. Now that's fun.

But the fun doesn't stop there. Jason's big into alerts. So when certain inventory levels get below a minimum, his purchasing guy gets an e-mail alert to order more. If a ship date passes the current date, then his customer service person gets an e-mail alert. If an inventory item hasn't been counted recently, his warehouse manager gets an alert. Jason takes alerts even to his receivables systems too. His controller gets email alerts when invoices go past 30 days. And if helium inventory levels are high, then Jason takes care of that too. He has a lot of fun doing that.

All of this is done by his accounting software. Most popular accounting applications do this stuff today. And most major databases, like Microsoft's SQL Server, allow you to write "triggers" which are the same as alerts. Knowing things before they happen is fun. Finding out after the fact isn't. Just ask the people who invested with Bernie Madoff.

Want more accounting software fun? Ask Susan.

Susan is a partner at a ten-person law firm. Sure, as an attorney she likes to eat puppies and beat little children. But there's another side to her too. A fun side. She's running a business. Susan doesn't have to worry about inventory. But she can still have fun with her accounting software.

There's a lot of stuff she needs to know about every day. Like unbilled time that needs to be billed. And pending client work that needs to be assigned. And client projects that are running up against their limits. Susan's not an accountant but that doesn't mean she doesn't know how to use her accounting software. She gets flash info.

Every day there's a Flash Report on her desk. This report is a one pager with key information about the firm. The flash info. Plus open receivables and open payables. She's not waiting for the end of the month to get her information. She's getting it immediately. She's taking advantage of the daily reports that her accounting system offers. Like alerts, most software today generates dashboards and flash reports and daily status information, in addition to the detailed financial stuff that accountants like to know.

Like Susan, Ellen's another owner who has fun with accounting software.

Ellen sees her accounting application as a sales tool. She runs one of those annoying franchise kiddie-tumbly-gymastic places. The ones that hand parents two Advil and a shot of Jack Daniels when entering. Every time Ellen sends out an invoice she plays with the message on the bottom. She advertises upcoming classes. She promotes her summer camps. She highlights a great staff member. Her invoices are like mini-tweets (there, now I'm cool because I just referenced Twitter). Ellen looks at her invoices not just as a bill for services, but as a communication with her customers. Fun!

Another fun thing I've seen good managers do: They beat up their accounting software partners. They have them come in, or get online, and demonstrate to them new features, add on applications, and better ways to use the product they have. They torture them with questions and try to soak some free training from them. The software vendors think they're going to sell upgrades or more licenses. Boy, are they naïve.

See? For a few smart managers, accounting applications can be fun! And profitable too!

Fearless Mike Knows How To Collect

In colonial times, men were men.

They hunted animals and dueled at dawn. They went weeks without showering. They lived for days off the land and spent their nights drinking whiskey.

I am not one of those men.

I hunt down good sushi bars and pull hamstrings playing softball on Sunday mornings. I never go more than a few days without showering. (Note to readers: Stay away from my house on the weekends.) I drink wine out of a box. I drive a minivan.

Mike Smaleren, my penny-pinching friend, however, is more of a man than I. He owns a 40-person carpentry company, works both inside and outside in bad weather, sometimes chews tobacco and drives a pickup truck. Whereas I'm afraid of what will happen if I mix red and white wine with my dinner, Mike is fearless - especially when it comes to his work.

Not all contractors are fearless like Fearless Mike. (Actually, I don't call him this name to his face because I'm afraid he'll punch me.)

For example, there's a lawsuit currently making its way through the federal and state court systems where a bunch of contractors are suing a general contractor who is, in turn, suing a steakhouse owner. No, it's not about a bad porterhouse. You guessed it: It's about money. Unpaid money to be more exact.

Seems like the contractors - painters, electricians and the like - did work for the general contractor and didn't get paid. And it seems like the general contractor didn't get paid by the steakhouse chain. Seems like a familiar story.

A total mess.

Haven't we learned? Why are contractors still chasing down money from their customers? People have been building stuff for thousands of years. Surely someone's figured out a way to just get paid on time and avoid these problems. Right?

Well, Fearless Mike has. Why? Because Fearless Mike, a true entrepreneur, has three principles when it comes to a job: Any changes get written up, payments need to be current and, most important, if things get out of the comfort zone, he walks.

The story behind the steakhouse lawsuit is that the contractors were forced to do a ton of work on a very short timetable. The job was a moving target. Sometimes there were written change orders. Other times, there weren't. The project managers were forced into doing more work with promises of payment. They were swept up into the project.

"Not my game," says Fearless Mike.

Fearless Mike doesn't like to do anything out of contract. If his men are asked to perform additional services, then he wants a written change order. "This is my protection," he says. And it's not such an unreasonable request. If a customer wants more work done, then Fearless Mike just likes to put it all in writing. Simple.

Fearless Mike also wants to see the cash. Most of his projects are done by milestone, or payment date. As long as he delivers what he promised, he expects payment to be made. "I'm not into giving a restaurant chain a line of credit," he says. "That's what banks are for." Easier said than done? Well, this is why Fearless Mike is so fearless - because Fearless Mike isn't afraid to stop.

"I know what my limits are," he says. "And if I reach that limit, I stop." By limits, Fearless Mike knows what his exposure is. He knows just how much he's willing to risk on a job, financially that is, before he's had his fill. Mike is willing to put a few bucks out there in payroll and materials. But if he's not getting money in soon enough, he's ready and willing to stop everything in its tracks and back away.

This takes a lot of courage. Walking away from a big job, particularly in a slow economy, is a bold thing to do. Some would say a little crazy. But Fearless Mike has a lot of confidence. Oh, and he also has some cash in the bank, too. "It's amazing how you can make these decisions when you know you've got that cushion," he says. Companies that are desperate for work may stretch themselves too far to please their customers. That may be OK some of the time. But in the steakhouse situation, this is not a good thing at all.

Does this make some people angry? Sometimes. Does he lose jobs? Occasionally. "But at least I'm not out suing people, like those poor knuckleheads and that steakhouse owner," he says.

Fearless Mike's words, not mine.

My words would be more harsh.

Fearless Mike has done good jobs for good people. He's sitting on cash and his business is financially sound. Like any good manager, he has no intention of rocking that boat just because of someone else's disorganization.

I'm too old to change certain things. I like to drink white wine. I'll never drive a pickup truck. And chewing tobacco just makes me ill.

But when it comes to getting paid on a future job, I'm going to take the advice of my penny-pinching friend, Fearless Mike. And I'll be prepared to walk away from projects that are too risky to keep working.

Collection Tips For The Wicked

Here is one thing all small business owners have in common: When we're in our 80s, sitting in our wet diapers at some run-down nursing home, addled with arthritis and beaten down with Alzheimer's disease, we'll still be able to remember (clear as day) every single deadbeat customer that stiffed us during the course of our business lives.

I hate most types of cheese, pro wrestling, slow drivers, girls' field hockey and those commercials with the cavemen in them. But most of all, I hate customers who don't pay our bills. I hate being put in a position to beg for something that's due. I hate having to feel like I'm the guy doing something wrong when it's really the deadbeat customers who owe me.

Collecting money takes extra time and effort. It's a pain in the butt. Especially when most of the time we spend collecting is from customers who know they owe us but just … don't feel like paying. Unbelievable.

A few smart business owners have taught me some tricks to help collect money faster. Although these have been helpful I've found that the best advice I've received is about the tactics that DON'T work, especially for small business.

For example, contracts don't help to collect money any faster. People read what they want to read. Just because it SAYS in your contract AND on your invoice that "all amounts are due in 30 days" is meaningless. Just because a customer signed a contract and is legally bound to the agreement is irrelevant. We all know that no one's going to court over a $1,000 invoice. Good managers know not to rely on written contracts to enforce an outstanding invoice. People often don't do what they say and just as often don't do what they're legally bound to do. Plan for that.

Want to put your customer at ease with a few good belly laughs? Bill him for finance charges. That always gets a hoot. Most of us crack up when, on occasion, one of our suppliers makes a pathetic attempt to lay on a finance charge for a late invoice. We know they're barely smart enough to figure out sales tax, let alone appreciate the "time value of money's" effect on their business.

Give me a break. Finance charges, unless you're the phone company, are a waste of time. If I'm masochistic enough to still do business with a late-paying client I build the "finance charges" into my hourly rates.

Collection experts tell us to check credit in advance. Do they also advise us where to find someone to do this for us and how to pay for their time? Citibank has plenty of credit checkers, I'm sure. But A&A Paving has Shirley doing the books and Miriam answering the phones. They're going to check credit? And with who? An incomplete and out of date Dun & Bradstreet report?

Even the guys that do take the time to check credit for a customer in advance know they're still taking a crapshot. Smart managers keep the credit checking to a minimum and make sure their accounts receivable exposure, especially with new customers, is kept at a low. Most of us know that it's probably cheaper to write off a few receivables during the year than invest the time and money to do credit-collection work.

Collection agencies are generally useless for small business too. They're expensive, taking 30 percent to 50 percent of what they collect for pretty much just writing letters.

A few customers may be frightened into paying, but they're the naïve ones.

Once the letter writing campaign is unsuccessful you'll be asked to pay legal fees to take it up to the next level. And then it just becomes cost-prohibitive. The lawyers always win in the end.

One nice thing about collection companies is that there is some sweet retribution knowing that a deadbeat customer is on the receiving end of a few nasty and threatening letters. Use a collection company sparingly and with low expectations.

The worst payers? Big companies by far. They take great joy in delaying your payment the minute you do something outside of their bureaucratic procedures. God forbid you send an invoice to the wrong person at a big company. It's the perfect reason to shuffle paperwork while your payment gets delayed. I find that big companies have super-formalized processes and procedures ... until something goes wrong. Then all systems shut down.

My invoice didn't have a purchase order number? Let the heavens rain down on my head! I am not worthy to be paid! If you're doing business with large companies, be extra careful to get your invoice to the right person and confirm that it's been officially entered into their system. Also make sure you've completed all of their paperwork (like a W-9) in advance too — that's another great way to delay payment too.

So what's the truth? The world is full of deadbeats. Every year you're going to have writeoffs. Expect it. Reserve for it. Try to keep it minimal. Don't think about it too much. At least you'll have some stories to share in your old age. Pampers anyone?

The 80% Factor

We live in a very imperfect world.

My cell phone drops calls about 10 times a week. My bacon at breakfast yesterday wasn't served well done like I asked. My flight last week was late. The roof of my Jeep has a small leak.

Imperfections are part of our life. Nothing works 100 percent. We're used to this in our personal lives. And, as business owners and managers, we're used to this in our professional lives, too.

We know all about imperfections. So as business owners, we make up for the imperfect business world by creating reserves on our financial statements. Good managers are constantly creating these reserves for the imperfections with our customers, vendors, products and services.

For example, it's not uncommon for 5 percent or 10 percent of a company's receivables to be reserved as potential bad debts. That's because some imperfect people who say they're going to pay ... don't. I know of some companies that have up to 20 percent of their inventory reserved as obsolete, or unsellable. That's because product that they purchased and expected to sell ... didn't. Other clients I know build a returns and allowances reserve of anywhere between 3 percent and 7 percent on sales. That's because product or services that they thought were good ... weren't.

Imperfections. The world is full of them.

As business owners and managers, we know this. Every business has its share of lousy customers, poorly made product or jobs that didn't go as hoped. No one's perfect. We're not going to get it all right all the time. At home, we can apologize and promise to not make that mistake again. In the business world, we do the same thing AND we pay to make it right. This financial impact is then reserved for on our balance sheets.

Mary Buckley also knows this. She calls this "The 80% Factor." It's a theory that she lives by daily. This is her emotional reserve. And it goes like this: "As long as 80 percent of my customers are happy, then I'm happy," Mary says.

Because Mary knows she's not perfect. She has corns on her feet. She doesn't recycle as often as she should. She admits to sometimes watching "Two And A Half Men." And her oldest child is a Republican. (Oops! So am I.)

More important, being a good manager, she knows that she can't make everyone happy. Her hair salon, located on a busy street, serves hundreds of customers every month. This may come as a surprise for some, but I've heard that a few women can be quite fussy about their hair. Just a rumor. But that's what I've heard.

Mary confirmed this suspicion. "There are times when we follow a customer's instructions and she's still not happy," Mary says. Sometimes you do everything you can do. But it's still not good enough.

Good managers reserve. Both financially and emotionally.

Financially, we're honest with our balance sheets. Bad receivables are reserved or written off. This way we can get this bad karma out of our heads and focus on the good receivables from the good customers. Unsellable inventory isn't left lying around. It's scrapped or disposed of. All it does is remind us of jobs gone bad, dreams that never happened. We don't need that kind of karma either. And let's face it, some of our products are going to be returned. A reasonable reserve should be set up so we don't get ourselves into an emotional state whenever a silly customer has a silly complaint. We return, we move on. We focus on the good.

Reserves are just a cost of doing business. Good business people understand this and plan for imperfections. That way when a customer doesn't pay, or a part doesn't work like it should, we've already absorbed the cost. Both financially and emotionally.

That's why Mary lives by The 80% Factor. She does her best. But she knows she's not going to make every customer happy. Instead of spinning her wheels on the 20 percent of customers who give her 80 percent of her headaches she instead spends the time on the 80 percent of her customers who give her 0 percent of her headaches.

"You want to please everyone," she says. "But you just can't. I don't let it bother me. I do my best. I sleep soundly. I watch 'Two and A Half Men.'" And she makes her reserves.

Say Hello To My Little Card

Who still uses cash? I stopped going to ATMs years ago. It was on doctor's orders. It seemed like I was always behind the 97-year-old lady who was orchestrating a takeover of the bank (either that or trying to remember her four-digit PIN). My body cannot physically deal with the stress of an ATM transaction. Or Mel's Diner either.

I don't go to Mel's Diner for the same reason that I don't go to ATMs. It's the closest diner to my house, but I go to another diner which is just a little farther down the road. Is it the food? Not really; a sandwich is a sandwich. The service? Not that either -- in fact, Mel's waitresses, Flo and Alice, are quite a hoot.

It's the cards. Mel's Diner only accepts cash. He won't take my debit card. And the other diner does.

I once asked Mel why he don't take credit or debit cards. "And pay their ridiculous fees? Forget it!" He yelled.

Well, for goodness sake, Mel, just pay the fees already.

Hold on! Did the "penny pincher" actually just say to PAY the card fees? I thought he was about saving money, pinching pennies, and all that kind of stuff.

Yes, saving money is important for any penny pincher. But the best business people I know also know that it's more important to spend their money wisely. Paying a transaction fee for a card service may help to generate a lot more business then requiring customers to pay cash.

How many other customers turn away from Mel's Diner because Mel doesn't take credit or debit cards? How many customers ordered a little less because they realized they didn't have enough cash on them? How many customers, as they're forced to search out a nearby ATM machine, grumble to themselves that they'll never return? How many times have Flo and Alice received lower tips because the customers didn't have the extra cash?

Maybe it's not just the fees. Maybe Mel is keeping things off the books so he can declare lower cash receipts and play around with his taxes. "Those card statements leave an audit trail," he says.

Gee, that's soooo smart! Like any Internal Revenue Service agent with a fifth-grade education couldn't monitor receipts at Mel's place for a few days and easily estimate his income.

If you're not accepting credit or debit cards then you could be throwing away money. Mel is missing out on sales. The supposed fees (or taxes) that he's saving are more likely less than the net profits he'd be getting by the added volume. No, he's not "saving" his customer's (that means me) money either, because we both know he's not charging them (me) any less than he would charge if they (I) were paying by a card. He's inconveniencing them (me) for his benefit. Even Alice and Flo would agree: he's just not providing a very good service for his customers. That's me.

Accepting a credit or debit card at your business is easy. It's done through third party services, like Merchantwarehouse. com or Open.com (they're part of American Express). They'll set you up with the machines, and of course charge you an arm and a leg too. Expect to pay a mind-numbing 2 to 3 percent on every transaction, plus the usual Draconian setup fees. And please, don't buy into their leasing deals. You'll wind up paying $89,000 for a $600 processing machine before you're all through.

Get ready for some credit checking too. The credit-card processors want to know who they're reimbursing. You may get an onsite visit and some questions about your business.

But good businesspeople suck it up. They pass the charges through to their customers if they can. They understand the big picture.

Sorry, Mel. I refuse to part with the few dollar bills I carry for your soggy club sandwich when I can get an equally soggy sandwich at your competitor down the street ... with my debit card. For now you can just kiss my grits!

How To Ruin A Job

My family and I suffered through a nightmare last spring. But it wasn't Joe's fault. Really.

Joe (his real name was José, but he told us to call him Joe) and his two assistants were part of the team that refinished the floors in our house. He was a nice enough guy. He couldn't understand much English. Or maybe he was pretending not to understand English. Especially when we were complaining. Man, did we do a lot of complaining during that miserable two-week period!

We complained because Joe and his team really screwed up our flooring job. My wife and I, plus our three less-than-hygienic teenage kids, spent the better part of those two weeks living out of one room together. There were large swathes of our house that were off-limits for hours during critical parts of the day. There were other areas that never seemed to be completed. There were a lot of toxic odors — some from the floor treatment fluids and the rest from my sons.

The job didn't go as planned. That really surprised us. We met two times with the company owner to plan out the phases. Things really came to a head one Saturday morning near the end of this nightmare when Joe breathlessly showed up unannounced at our door.

"My boss is coming to inspect the job — please don't tell him about our problems or I will be fired!" Not wanting to be the cause of further unemployment in the area (we'll leave that up to the Federal Reserve) my wife called the owner and rescheduled his visit. The whole thing was awkward and left an unpleasant feeling. Why was Joe so terrified of this guy?

Joe wasn't really at fault for this debacle. He's just the guy who does the work. The real culprit here was the boss. He was the one who originally estimated the job. He was the one ultimately responsible for the job's outcome. He did a lousy job managing this job. His lack of oversight caused extra labor costs. He was left with an unhappy customer who would never use his company again.

Over the two-week period that Joe and his team were working on our floors, the boss visited the job site … never. Even when I called, asking why things were behind schedule and why certain rooms were being done out of sequence, I was directed to his scheduling person. He wouldn't even take my calls. He was never around. And the scheduling lady, like Joe, was on the defense. She too seemed fearful of retribution. The big bad boss, the business owner, was managing through fear and failing. This is not a good combination.

The owner never seemed to check in with Joe. He seemed comfortable communicating the job plans to a man that couldn't speak English and then just letting him roll. Conscientious managers don't do this. We try to be intimately familiar with a job while it's going on. Every minute is costing us money. Any deviation from plan can drain cash from our budget. Physically stopping by the job site is always worth the time. The boss never appeared at our house during this fiasco and now he's paying the price. There's no way that this job was as profitable as he was expecting. Even with the sub-minimum-under-the-table wages he's no doubt paying his team.

The whole fear of the boss thing seemed a little much too. In my company, we always have problems. No job is ever perfect. You have to expect these things. Barking and growling and scaring your employees leads to cover-ups and backpedaling. None of his people wanted to take ownership of a problem. There was always finger-pointing. I, the customer, suffered because of this.

And here's the final kicker: it's been months since the job completed and have I heard from the boss? Nope. Not a call. Not an e-mail. Not a fruit basket. Believe it or not, Joe did a pretty good job in the end. Our floors look nice. A cordial conversation with the company's owner would have probably smoothed things over. I'm a business owner. I understand that stuff happens. I live in a community where people are always looking for contractors too.

But this guy doesn't seem to care about this. I guess he's on to the next job. And I'm left feeling … annoyed.

Finished? Now Bill!

How did Jane get a free night at a four-star hotel?

Jane is partner in charge of a six-person engineering firm and a client of ours. "I always seem short of cash," she once complained to me. "We seem to be doing fine," she said. "I've got plenty of work and good clients, but when it comes to pay my bills I'm juggling, juggling, juggling!"

It only took a few minutes to figure this one out. Jane's bookkeeper waited until the end of the month before invoicing customers. This practice was to "make the accounting easier." In reality, the billing was killing her! Jane's billing system favored everyone ... but Jane.

By the time she got all the paperwork together, her invoices weren't going out the door until the end of the first week of the new month. Some of these contained charges for work performed more than 30 days ago. And, of course, few of Jane's clients actually paid their invoices under 30 days.

In fact, some of them were receiving invoices so long after the fact that they suffered what I called "temporary accounts payable amnesia." This is a common affliction suffered by hundreds of thousands of business owners and managers who "kind of forget" that the services had been "actually performed" and that they "actually owed money" for them.

As a result, many invoices went past 30 days due, causing Jane to use her vast medical training (and a guy named Vito) in order to "cure" these clients of this "amnesia" and get them to pay.

The end result is that a good portion of her invoices were getting paid 60 to 90 days after the services were done. And it's not like Jane was withholding payroll until she collected from her clients. Her engineers got their money weeks ago. No wonder Jane feels like there's never enough in her account.

Jane had a revelation. Why not bill her invoices at the end of each week instead of at the end of each month? Brilliant! But not perfect. Even waiting until the end of the week costs her money. Billing needs to be done immediately.

A smart manager realizes that once a service is performed or a product is shipped, she's owed money.

She also knows that her customers aren't going to knock on her door and throw money in her face. In fact, they'll conveniently forget that they ever bought anything from her unless she sends them an invoice to remind them. That "reminder" needs to go out as soon as possible. She also knows that the clock for paying in 30 days will begin, for most customers, when they receive the invoice, regardless of the invoice date.

Get your invoices out immediately. Start the collection process right away. You can't be a good negotiator unless you're dealing from a position of strength. You won't be dealing from a position of strength unless you've got a good amount of cash in the bank that makes you feel strong.

Savings? Assume that Jane mails 100 invoices a month and each invoice averages $1000. At a 4 percent annual interest rate, she's losing 11 cents per day per invoice. By speeding things up only three days, Jane pocketed $396 this year ... and paid for a fancy-shmancy room at the Four Seasons!

How Much Money Did You Lose Today?

Psst! Want to make an extra $5,000 to $10,000 next year?

No, this isn't an advertisement to do telemarketing from your home, or even one of those great investment "tips" you keep receiving in your e-mail inbox.

This is all about having someone in your office take about 30 minutes each day so that they can tell you how much money you made (or lost) on the jobs that shipped out the day before.

It's easy. It's common sense. So naturally many of us don't do this. But if you're in the service, manufacturing or distribution businesses you're really letting some dollars slip away.

Here's what you do:

• Take out your payroll register from last year (and try not to get upset when you're reminded how much you're overpaying some people). Add up all the hours spent last year by your production and service employees.

• Next, take out last year's tax returns (and also try not to get upset over how you're overpaying) and add up all the overhead expenses you incurred last year, like utilities, maintenance, office expenses, etc.

• Now divide the overhead expenses by hours to come up with an overhead rate per hour.

• Finally: create a little spreadsheet. Have an admin person in your office find out the cost of materials used and the time spent for each job that shipped the day before. This is not a tough assignment as long as your admin person knows how to use a phone. Have that person enter this information plus the selling price and shipping cost on a pre-designed spreadsheet that includes the overhead rate per hour. Let the spreadsheet calculate profit.

Get a copy of that spreadsheet every single day! Every ... single ... day! And start getting surprised.

Some jobs (or products, or classes, or services, or projects) that you thought were making money didn't make as much. Other jobs may have been more profitable than you estimated. Many probably came in line with what you expected.

Now you can make your adjustments.

It's not perfect. The numbers probably aren't exact. Some time incurred may be mischarged. Some of the overhead expenses or hours may have changed a bit. But it's going to be pretty close. And it's also not a six-figure job-costing system that some consultants would recommend. Plus you're going to find it interesting.

• You may find yourself getting reacquainted with your production people and your customers.

• You may be relieved to get rid of those customers that you always suspected were unprofitable.

• You may find yourself taking advantage of some vendors that for years were taking advantage of you.

Want help setting this up? Ask your accountant. In fact, your accountant should have already made this suggestion. If not, maybe it's time to find a new one.

How did I come up with a $5,000-$10,000 savings? If you bill out half a million or a million a year, and you grow your job profits by just 1 percent, there's your answer.

Great management starts with each job going out the door. Time to warm up that spreadsheet!

Financial Statements Can Be Useless

I have a friend, Josh, who wastes way too much time with his financial statements. Josh runs a 50-person company. He does 100 jobs a month and maybe writes 200 or so checks. But his accountant tells him that he should be reviewing a monthly balance sheet, income and cash-flow statement. (Surprise! Guess who gets paid to put these together for him?)

Most financial statements for small companies are useless. Accountants and textbooks and software companies and business gurus all say they're so important. They're not. They're a waste of time. These people are just trying to sell business owners like Josh their own agenda, like buying services, books and software from them.

Smart business people don't buy into this baloney.

For example: cash. Josh should make sure he knows how much is in the bank and how much is showing on his books. He should get it reconciled each month by someone outside of his company (for example, a temp or a college accounting student). Then he should look at the reconciliation to make sure there's nothing unusual passing through.

He should know what he's owed and what he owes. He should keep track of his open receivables and payables. This will tell him everything he wants to know about how his business is doing. More is usually good, as long as it's under control. We should all put down the sports page and read our receivables aging every two weeks to keep on top

213

of our inevitable deadbeat customers who promise to pay and then don't.

Two more critical numbers Josh should track: backlog and pipeline. Backlog meaning orders he's received but hasn't shipped out the door. Pipeline meaning orders he hopes to receive because there are quotes outstanding. Josh needs to make sure he's getting these reports every week and reading them.

What about productivity? It would be good for Josh to know how many people were out this week. Or how many overtime hours were spent. Or even the total labor hours recorded so far this week.

These are not your typical financial statements. Josh's accountant may get excited by comparing monthly expenses with last month's expenses. But this is past history. It's OK to do this every six months or so, but it's not necessary to do it very often. Cutoff won't be great, so there'll inevitably be fluctuations month to month. For a small company it's better to spot trends over a longer period of time. Josh needs to tell his accountant to find something else to do with his time, like figuring out how to reduce his tax bill (or getting his thrills somewhere else).

There is one thing a smart manager can do that's accounting-like, but useful. Read your general ledger. You're not Exxon Corp., so your detailed general ledger report won't be that big. Print it out each month, sit down one morning (preferably near a bathroom, as you can never know your reaction to some of these things) and just page through it. Here you'll really see the nuts and bolts of everything going through your company. If you're a good businessperson then you should recognize just about all the transactions. If anything raises an eyebrow then go and raise hell. You'll learn more by reading your general ledger then any other financial statement.

Every day, Josh should have his office manager cut short

her "Days Of Our Lives" break for five minutes and put all of these numbers (cash, receivables, payables, backlog, pipeline) on a single piece of paper and call it his Daily Flash Report. I mentioned this in a previous chapter. She should make sure it's on his desk when he strolls in every morning at 11 after golf. Josh can get the detail reports backing up these numbers only when he needs them.

What's the payback? More control. Better management of the key numbers. Getting this report should be an exercise in validation. Good managers will use these numbers as a gut check to help them make their decisions.

Want Better Info? Try A Balanced Scorecard

Ever try to keep a scorecard at a little league baseball game? After a while, you learn to track what's most important, ignore the niggling errors and just make sure there's a snack at the end. Well-managed businesses--large and small--use a similar approach.

The concept of managing by "balanced scorecard" has been around awhile. It boosts performance using a combination of metrics, goals and process improvements. The U.S. Navy, City of Newark and the Atlanta Public School System are just a few large organizations that have benefited from this approach. Many businesses can too.

First step: Establish certain key metrics for success--from both operating and financial points of view. Key operating metrics might run the gamut from production lead times to monthly scrap allowance; financial indicators might include revenue and earnings growth, asset turnover, balance sheet leverage, and most important of all, cash flow. (When coming up with financial metrics, make sure to capture performance from three perspectives, as recorded in your company's income statement, balance sheet and cash flow statement. Each one tells a different story.) Next, draw up a "scorecard" to track results and changes over time.

"The big thing that a balanced-scorecard approach does is that it helps management focus on strategy and results instead of tasks," says Howard Rohm, chief executive of the Balanced

Scorecard Institute, a nonprofit consulting firm. "When effectively implemented, companies improve performance by measuring what matters and prioritizing work."

Balfour Beatty, a $2.4 billion (sales) construction firm headquartered in Dallas is in the balanced-scorecard big leagues. "All of our scorecards are structured around people, process, customers and financials," says John Parolisi, a senior vice president at the company.

Parolisi uses multiple scorecards, each drilling down on a different aspect of the business. Each scorecard lays out 2-to-4 strategic objectives and 1-to-3 metrics per objective-- so 2-to-12 metrics per card. "For example, we have a process objective called 'consistently deliver the signature experience' where we measure customer satisfaction through surveys," says Parolisi. "This is a critical metric for us." Other key metrics could include employee turnover rates or on-time delivery performance.

For many of us, Balfour's complex metric-management system is probably overkill. We'd do just as well with a little league version.

Alex Phinn takes this approach. Phinn, a little league coach, is also president of Griff Paper and Film, a 50-person manufacturer and distributor of protective films, silicone-coated liners and specialty labeling materials in Pennsylvania. Phinn started with a sheet of paper and chose a handful of important operating and financial metrics, including, open purchase orders and open quotes, as well as daily receivables, payables, cash balance and year-to-date sales (vs. the prior year). He also threw in some other tell-tale performance and quality indicators, like the number of employee absentee days and customer complaint calls. Phinn peruses these numbers every day over his morning coffee.

While large companies need all kinds of sign-offs to implement a detailed scorecard approach, the lighter flashcard

217

version is easy to install for small business owners. Says Phinn: "Once my three brothers and I signed on to the daily flash report, we had all the executive approval needed."

Phinn isn't buying special Balanced Scorecard software (and there's plenty of it out there), nor is he hiring a lot of expensive consultants (there are plenty of them out there too). He's doing today what will make him quicker, better, wiser-- and richer--tomorrow.

Ever Check These Numbers? You Should

How do you know if a pitcher is having a good season on the mound for the Milwaukee Brewers? A typical baseball fan might point to his record like a 4.69 earned run average and conclude it's been mediocre at best.

But look at the numbers a little deeper, and a different story emerges. While short on wins, the pitcher's 1.16 "WHIP"--that is, walks and hits per inning pitched--is strong.

Like savvy coaches, savvy entrepreneurs mind their stores using a flurry of metrics. Some are obvious--things like revenues, gross profit margin and dollars of scrap--but many others aren't (or at least they're not monitored). And while you don't have to be a Wall Street securities analyst to run a successful small business, having a handle on these numbers can make a huge difference--both in day-to-day management and in long-term planning.

Here are a few examples, in no particular order.

Cash Flow From Operations

Net income is nice, but cash flow is truly sweet. While the first is an abstract accounting measure, the second reflects the hard reality of how much cold currency is flowing into and out of a company.

The cash flow statement is a marriage of two other financial statements: the income statement (which tallies revenues and expenses) and the balance sheet (which records

219

"working capital" accounts, such as receivables and payables).

Example: Say your business has revenues of $1,000 for a given month, but all the merchandise was sold on credit (meaning that you didn't actually receive the cash in that period). Now say total cash outlays were $750 for the period. In this case, your income statement would report a "profit" of $250 ($1,000 in total revenues less $750 in expenses). Meanwhile, however, cash flow dropped by $750. That's because the business had to pay $750 in cash expenses but did not collect any offsetting cash from customers. An increase of $1,000 to accounts receivable balances the books.

The specific metric to watch: cash flow from operations (as opposed to cash from financings or investment income). Operating cash flow represents how much cash the company generates from its core operations--essentially, how well its heart is pumping. The calculation: net income plus depreciation and amortization (both non-cash charges), minus capital expenditures (new equipment and such), minus changes in working capital. One other important thing about cash flow: It is the metric generally used by investment bankers to determine the value of your company.

Inventory Turns

The longer stuff sits on a company's shelves, the lower the rate of return on those assets and the greater their vulnerability to falling prices. That's why you want to keep your inventory moving, or "turning." To calculate inventory turns, divide revenues by the average inventory level (in dollars) over the given accounting period. The greater the ratio (or number of turns), the greater the return on your capital. (An alternative method: Change the numerator to "cost of goods sold" and divide by inventory; this maneuver accounts for the fact that inventories are carried on your balance sheet at the original purchase price, while revenues are recorded at current market value.)

Receivables Growth Vs. Sales Growth

Relax--it's OK if receivables pile up a bit, as long as they grow proportionally with sales. If receivables begin to outstrip revenues, then you aren't getting paid--meaning that you might be short on cash when you need it most.

On-time Deliveries

Nothing stings worse than losing the trust and respect of your customers--and that's exactly what happens when you blow a delivery date. Missed dates should be flagged and investigated. The snafus may be flukes; then again, you may uncover a nagging flaw in the system. Like any other metric, track delivery trends over time.

Backlog

Sales may be brisk this week, but how will they look 90 days from now? Tracking this forward-looking metric-- defined as committed orders plus forecast sales, weighted by the probability of landing those deals--ensures that you're not running right off a cliff.

Interest Rate Coverage

No matter the credit environment, the answer to whether your company can consistently generate enough income to cover interest on borrowed money is a need-to-know item for lenders. There are many ways to define an interest-coverage ratio, but a common one is earnings before interest and taxes (or EBIT), divided by interest expense. Banks take this metric very seriously--so should you.

Every industry (and company within it) has its own set of meaningful metrics. Choose ones that capture performance from all three perspectives--in terms of income, leverage and cash flow--and track them week-in and week-out. Remember that each number tells a different story, and only taken together do they deliver what all smart owners ultimately crave: honesty.

Tali Perlstein complains all the time. Every time I talk to her it's always something. Taxes are too high. Sales are too low. Her husband's record collection takes up too much space. It seems like there's always something that's making her unhappy. Then it was the accounting system we sold her.

"I can't get any useful information from this system," she barked at me one day a few months ago. "The reports are just terrible."

The troubling thing was that I agreed with her. Tali may complain a lot, but she's usually not too far off the mark. Taxes are too high. Her husband does spend too much money on old records. And most software applications have lousy report writers.

Tali needs her reports. An income statement at the end of the year just isn't enough. She needs better information more frequently. She wants to know how much she shipped yesterday and to whom. She wants to keep track of her open purchase orders. She wants to know if her year-to-date-sales are ahead or behind last year. She needs to be alerted if overtime hours are out of control. She wants to know how many overpriced records her husband bought last month. It's not as if the information isn't in the system. It is. Well, most of it anyway. It's just that getting it out isn't easy.

"It's like pulling teeth!" she growls.

She's right to complain. Sure, most business software products have a list of standard reports. But they're just that -- standard. Everyone's business is unique in some way and just about every business person I know is like Tali. They want specialized reports for their purposes. They may not complain as much. But their desires are the same.

I told Tali that she needs to make a decision. Take action or cut the complaining. Yes, the report writer stinks. Most of them do. But there is a solution. She can hire someone to write the reports she needs. A good manager, Tali at first wasn't crazy about that either.

"Why should I pay someone to do what the software should do for me already?"

That was an easy one to answer. She already pays a landscaper to mow her lawn because her husband doesn't want to do it. She pays a plumber to fix a leak because her husband isn't capable of doing it. If she could hire someone to replace her husband in ... well, you get the point. This is nothing different.

Tali bit the bullet. She hired a consultant to come in for a few days and create the special reports she needed. He quoted her $2,500 to do the reports. She complained bitterly. But in the end she caved. And he got to work.

Within weeks, she knew she had made a good decision. Using the new reports she found herself having a better handle on the business. She took action when sales lagged. She jumped all over her vendors when purchase orders became overdue. She tracked her largest customers and made calls when their orders were less than expected. Lost sales were found. Wayward expenses were reined in.

When the time came to pay Tali happily wrote the check. Was it because she was pleased with the investment? Partly. But the real reason? She actually raised the money through a very special sale. So in the end these extra reports didn't cost her a thing.

And as for her husband, I doubt he'll ever miss those stupid old records.

26 People Who Lied To Me

Want to own a small business? It's not as romantic as you may think. Very few entrepreneurs go on to become the CEO's of publicly held companies. Sure, there are many upsides: the independence, the freedom, the joy of innovation, the girls, the parties, the cheering crowds. But for most of us, running a business means long hours of hard work in industrial parks near the airport. We deal with a lot of headaches. And boy, do we hear a lot of lies! Don't believe me? OK, then here's just a partial list of 27 people who lied to me this past week alone.

1. My banker. My banker personally assured me that I was a "very important customer" as I sat in his branch office. Umm...really? Aren't you the fifth guy I've seen sitting in that chair over the past six months? And aren't you feeling a little uncomfortable saying how valuable I am when your own office has no personal effects...anywhere? I'll start believing you if you're even still working at this bank the next time I visit. And by the way: do you know what my business actually does? I didn't think so.

2. The customer who told me he'll pay. Oh, those silly gooses. They always say that. And then 60 days later I have to call and beg them for the money owed to me from a service I already performed. And then I'm the devil and accused of "poor customer service" because I refuse to provide more services until the open invoice is paid. This happened to me last week. Footnote one week later: invoice is still unpaid.

3. The vendor who says he'll deliver on time. No he didn't. He forgot to tell me they were closed Monday for the holiday. Other than government workers and school teachers, since when is "President's Day" a holiday? Suffice it to say, the items I needed didn't arrive until the day after he promised. Why do I keep believing these guys?

4. My teenage daughter. I'm not sure what it is, but she lied to me about something last week. Just you wait and see.

5. The customer who told me "money's no object." Why, that's awesome! Then I'm raising my rates to $5,000.00 per hour. Oh, that's too expensive? Then I guess it is about the money. So...can we please stop saying that?

6. The guy who promised me more business. I love guys like that. "Yeah, give me a special deal now because there's LOTS more business where that came from." Here's what I learned in the past 18 years of running a business: I'm likely to grow more hair before I see more business from the guy who makes that promise.

7. The guy who invented those 5 Hour Energy drinks. Running a small business can be tiring, so who can resist a little energy shot in the middle of the afternoon, right? Wrong. All I experienced from one of these bottles was a case of the jitters and an overwhelming desire to drink human blood. Luckily, the jitters went away after only a few minutes.

8. Dun & Bradstreet. They, like many of their fellow credit bureaus, collect and sell financial data about businesses. They also determine the credit worthiness of our country's major banks. Last week, they assured me that the new customer of mine was a good credit risk. Anyone want to take bets?

9. The President. I'm warning you...do not believe his March Madness predictions: they're always wrong. Oh, and don't believe his claim that the payroll tax cut will help the economy. Tax "rebates" offered to the masses over the years have never worked. But they do make for tasty election year treats.

10. Rick Santorum. He wants us to spend more time with our families. That has to be a lie. Has he ever spent more than five minutes with a couple of teenagers? Has he never watched an episode of Gossip Girl?

11. Gallup. Their latest poll last week reported that our "economic confidence" is the best in a year. Well, let me check my bank account. Oh, cash is down. And my customers are still sitting on quotes and taking a "wait and see" attitude. Other than the makers of the "The Amazing Spiderman" (which looks...awesome!) is there anyone else feeling so confident about 2012?

12. The price of that new router for my home office. No, it wasn't $129.00 like I was promised. It wound up costing me $3,129.00. That would be the cost of the router plus the 15 hours of my time spent over the weekend trying to figure out why it was always going offline and why my wireless printers couldn't connect to it. (epilogue: router now working, wireless printers inexplicably go offline)

13. Charlie Manuel. He's lying when he says he wants to "adjust Ryan Howard at the plate." Any Phillies fan will tell you what he means to say is "when an opponent shifts every single one of their players to right field, we want Ryan to hit the ball to left field because if he keeps hitting like he's been hitting our fans will kill him."

14. Plug and play. That's a lie. Particularly when it came to the new bluetooth headset I purchased for my Dell desktop. There was plugging, but no playing. Instead there was lots of downloading, reinstalling, cursing, stomping, screaming and overseas calls to tech support where it was finally resolved.

15. The US Airways pilot on my flight to Orlando. He said that congestion at the Philadelphia airport would only delay us 10 minutes. Dude, have you ever flown out of the Philadelphia airport? It's never less than a 45 minute delay if you don't leave your gate on time and even then it's a good 30 minutes. But you knew that, didn't you?

16. My CPA. He lied to me when he promised to have this year's tax returns done in "a jiffy." A "jiffy" to most accountants means getting a Fedex delivered to your house at 11PM on April 14th. And God forbid if you have a question on what was done at that hour. But I'm sure he'll stand loyally by side in case there's an audit. Right? Hello? Hello?

17. The economists on Seekingalpha.com. Those guys seem so smart, don't they? And they all have their opinions about where the economy is going. And yet, they all seem to differ from one another. So who's lying to me? Who cares – most of them are usually wrong anyway.

18. The researchers in Australia who say that "work is causing cancer." Yeah, yeah. And so does alcohol, baby food, bottled water, celery, Adam Sandler movies, fruit, gingerbread, mobile phones and orange juice. We all know there's only one thing on that list that can truly cause cancer (or at least a very severe case of boredom). Now can we all just get back to work?

19. My "loyal" employee. He says he is. But he's not. Watch what happens when the economy gets better. We try to keep these people. But if they're really good, they get snapped up by Google or Microsoft anyway. Such is the life of a small business owner.

20. The company that sold me 10,000 prospects for my marketing campaign. They said the data was good. But when 8,000 emails get returned undelivered I have to question their claim. And I would, if their phone wasn't suddenly disconnected.

21. The guy who told me he was giving me the "best price". No it's not. It's the best price for him. Whenever someone says he's giving me his "best price" I know I'm being lied to. And in this case, I was. Because it was the same guy who sold me that list of 10,000 prospects. Drat!

22. The French. No one from France lied to me this past week. But I'm sure they would if they had the opportunity.

23. The search engine optimization consultant. Well, he didn't actually lie to me. Not exactly. He said that for $5,000 my company could be listed on the first page of Google. And it was. At 3AM Tuesday night. For 30 seconds. And then it disappeared into oblivion. Just like my five thousand bucks.

24. My IT guy. Either he lied, or he conveniently forgot to tell me that moving to "the cloud" would mean that it now takes five minutes to print out a document and five times as long to update a proposal in Word because of the slower performance. Oh, and my cloud server "doesn't support" internet browsing. So now I'm writing my letters and surfing the web from my desktop. Didn't I start there?

25. MakeUseOf's List of "inspirational" videos. What, after hearing all these lies you think I can get inspired? Where's a 5 Hour Energy Drink when you need one?

26. The U.S. Energy Information Administration. Last week they said we would become "more energy independent" by 2035. I never believe the predictions of any government agency. Not when they can't even figure out historical numbers without revising them 57 times. And uh...if we're becoming so energy independent why are my company's fuel costs higher than ever?

And the one person who didn't lie to me last week? The teenage girl at my local Starbucks who took my order with a bored expression, never looked me in the eye and handed me my coffee like it was a plastic bag of doggie doo. She could care less about me. No, I would never hire someone like her to work for me. But hey...at least she was honest!

Business Lessons From The British

My wife of 22 years is British and has endured much abuse from myself and my kids. Over the course of countless visits to her family in northwest London over the past two decades, she's heard all the jokes about the bad food, the bad teeth and the bad weather. Back at home, she's often forced to explain to our friends what a loo is, has to repeat words to adults who can't decipher her accent and is able to clear out an entire room full of people just by whipping out a jar of Marmite and a butter knife. Being British, particularly amongst a family of the ugliest of Americans, has not been easy for this poor woman. And then came the Olympics. And so we came to London to enjoy this once-in-a-lifetime event with our three teenage kids and their three teenage friends. We went to basketball, soccer, beach volleyball, badminton and other events.

And you know what? Wow. That's what.

We were amazed by the Olympic Park. We were impressed by the organization. And mostly we were overwhelmed by the British themselves. We normally see them grimly shuffling to work, swearing at their athletes and enduring the challenges of living in London. But the Olympics has put them in a different light. Despite what you may have been hearing in the media, we've watched an entire country of volunteers and organizers enthusiastically come together to pull off an amazing feat: hosting the world, cheering for Team GB, having a good time and putting on a fantastic show.

230

The British taught me a few things that week. And I am taking these lessons back to my business in America.

For example, I've learned to spend a few pence to save a few pounds. When we received our Olympic tickets a few months ago we also received a London Transport travel card for each day. This seemed to me a little strange. Until I got to London. And then I saw the brilliance. Because if we, along with every other ignorant American and tourist had to figure out their fare system and buy Tube tickets for each day the lines would've probably stretched to France. Some very, very smart and obscure British person somewhere figured this out. I'm sure that person ran into headwinds too. "What, just GIVE everyone a Tube ticket?" I can hear the critics say in that accent reserved exclusively for Hollywood villains. That brilliant person figured out that the money spent on transport tickets would save organizers millions in bad public relations and unhappy customers. And they're right. We've been minding the gap all week with no complaints whatsoever. To save, you must spend. And sometimes even an intangible return on investment might be more valuable than you think.

Next, always make sure you order enough crisps. Tearing ourselves away one morning from the riveting basketball game between Tunisia and Nigeria (and in case you were sitting on the edge of your seat, Nigeria won), my wife and I ran down to the concession stand for a coffee and found that the coffee stand was...out of coffee. And out of crisps too (which is probably a good thing because eating a packet of prawn cocktail crisps at nine in the morning is recommended only for the hardiest of British foodies...or the mentally ill). At lunchtime that day we decided to risk it and get a salt beef sandwich on rye bread with pickles. Except they were out of rye bread. And pickles. These are not big things, but I overhead many people grumbling about this. It's amazing how you can spend billions to erect an amazing facility and still upset people because they can't get a pickle with their sandwich. The details really are important. Sweat them.

And so what if you're quirky and you like Mr. Bean? Rowan Atkinson, the guy who plays Mr. Bean, is an Oxford educated electrical engineering major. And he was hilarious during the opening ceremonies. The British like to laugh at themselves. Among their top selling magazines are Private Eye and one of their most popular TV shows is Russell Howard's Good News, a current events satire. Their biggest selling newspaper unabashedly posts a bare-chested 21 year old beauty (not that I would...ahem...know about this, of course). The point of their opening ceremonies was not to wow the world with Chinese technology or American Hollywood effects. It was to say to the world "hey, we're British, we've contributed plenty to the world, we're proud of ourselves and we don't care if you don't think it's very funny to watch the Queen jump out of a helicopter...we do." In other words, if you believe in yourself and your company, don't pay attention to the critics. Just do it. And to hell with everyone else. Great innovators and successful business people have this kind of self-confidence. And I bet many of them also think Mr. Bean is hilarious.

And speaking of Mr. Bean, there have already been tons of mistakes. For example, "during a mass celebratory bell-ringing to mark the start of the games, Olympics Secretary Jeremy Hunt's bell went flying off its handle and narrowly avoided a bystander." Despite being sold-out, many events were showing empty premium seats on TV (that is until British military guys were allowed to attend and, given their choice of events, immediately flocked to...a women's beach volleyball match. Can I get a huzzah?) A mysterious woman walked along with the Indian athletic delegation without authorization. The keys were lost to Wembley Stadium. And when organizers mistakenly showed the South Korean flag when introducing the North Korean women's soccer team (note to self: they are bitter enemies and still technically at war) one enterprising small business owner, an optician, "ran a full-page ad displaying the two completely different-looking Korean flags and suggesting that anyone who can't tell the difference should stop by for a checkup." As a visitor here in London I watched organizers absorb the media abuse, make adjustments and move on. When launching a product, starting a project, hiring a new person, expanding a business you're going to make mistakes. People are going to criticize. Take a lesson from London: laugh, learn, adjust and carry forward.

In this world of mobile phones, social media and cloud based computing we've been told that the great companies are the ones maximizing profitability by minimizing their people and investing in technology. But here it's a different story. Sure, the Olympic organizers are using plenty of technology to pull off this huge event. But from the moment you arrive at Heathrow, to getting on the Tube, to arriving at the complex, to walking to your event...it's the people who are making it happen. People in brightly colored shirts smiling and pointing you the right way. Soldiers with guns ready ensuring our security (and my wife's adoring gaze). Workers efficiently dealing with the queues and the questions and the kids. Entertainers and dancers keeping us occupied between events. There's no technology here. Just people. And it reminds me that in my company, despite all the hype about technology, it's my people who will make me successful. That's surely the case here.

Most importantly, I want to be more like Beckham. What, like that guy isn't a total boss? Watching him speedboat alone down the Thames carrying the Olympic torch as fireworks exploded around him made me fantasize, very briefly, what it would be like to be married to this man. Beckham is cool and capable and was the right guy for the job. His confidence is infectious. You'd never know that a billion people were watching him and that anything could've happened to screw up his journey to the stadium (this IS England, you know). Am

I that cool and capable with my clients? Am I confident? Do I make them feel confident in my abilities? Am I a super-rich, super famous soccer player with a hot wife who used to be in the Spice Girls? No, I'm a middle class, slightly overweight, former accountant who looks more like George Costanza than a professional athlete. But my clients don't have to know these thoughts. They're hiring me to do a job and I'll do it confidently like Beckham.

I've learned plenty of things during my Olympics week in London. I've learned how to tell a young child how to "shut up" in 17 different languages. I've learned that Cricket is truly more boring than baseball. I've learned to look right when I cross the street. I've learned to love PG Tips Tea, Cadbury Flake and tuna fish sandwiches with butter. Most importantly I've learned a few lessons for running my business better when I return home. And for that, Great Britain, I thank you.

Hello, I Am An Outsourceaholic

Hello. My name is Gene Marks. And I am an outsourceaholic.

In this political environment it's embarrassing to admit my habit. I frequently hang out with other outsourcers. I know according to some these people are a bad influence on me and America. But it's a well known secret that there are many outsourceaholics like me who binge on outsourcing. This is an unspoken epidemic in this country. For many of us outsourcing is a quick high and a way to feel...oh, I don't know...cool and (dare I say it) profitable. I do a lot of outsourcing at nights and on the weekends, because the people who I outsource with (particularly in my industry) work this way. I selfishly hoard my best outsourcers from my friends so I can have them all to myself. I frequently pass out from the excitement of making money from outsourcing. Yes, I have employees. But in my heart I'm an outsourceaholic. It is an addiction. And I see no cure. Why would I want to be cured of this anyway? It's just too appealing.

For example, when I outsource I pay less taxes. I get this unique rush because I'm not hiring them as an employee. So that means that I'm not subject to certain employer related taxes, the most significant being the matching FICA and Medicare tax on their earnings. For 2012, the FICA tax is 4.2% (and is scheduled return to its prior 6.2% in 2013) on an employee's earnings up to $110,000. And the Medicare

Tax is 1.45% (also going up next year). As you can imagine, the authorities aren't crazy about this, so I've got to be very careful about where and how often I outsource. And I follow these very strict guidelines from the IRS just to be sure.

I don't have to pay other benefits too. Not paying taxes is one thing. Not paying other benefits makes me want to keep the party going. Subcontractors don't need healthcare, vacation, sick days, jury duty, 401K matches, disability insurance, membership to health clubs or car allowances. They don't require life insurance, child care subsidies, bonuses, adoption assistance, healthy snacks in the lunchroom. They don't require lunchroom either. These lower demands fuel my outsourcing addiction.

And my addiction costs even less because I don't have to include subcontractors on any tax filings and I don't have to track their year to date wages and taxes and other withholdings. I don't have to get my payroll service company involved. My bookkeeper doesn't have to keep separate paperwork on their benefits, taxes and child support payments. We don't need to track vacation and sick days. And we certainly don't have to liaise with any unions. Our subcontractors send us an invoice and if it's approved we pay in our normal weekly check runs. No habit it clean. But the outsourcing habit is.

I avoid unnecessary overhead too. I'm lucky enough to be in the technology business where I can feed my habit from my home office. My company is completely virtual. Therefore I have very low utilities, phone and Internet costs. I don't have to worry as much about insurance, auto expenses, continuing education, office supplies, office equipment, repairs, maintenance, trash removal and the inevitable downtimes that occur over the summer and Christmas holidays.

As an outsourceaholic I can enjoy just about any type

of outsourcing I can get. And I can be picky if I want to be. This means that when I need a developer who specializes in mobile applications for the iPad I hire that person to do the job. When I need help with telemarketing I hire a person with that skill set. I don't have to resort to synthetic or copycat solutions. By outsourcing I get the real deal.

I can easily find my contractors too. In the past I had to make much more of an effort because all I could do was take out an ad in a local newspaper. Today, I can find that specific expert where he or she lives by going online at great sites designed for that purpose. But it's a two way street. "If you want to find someone great, you must be a great client too." Says Fabio Rosati, CEO of Elance, an online platform that connects independent professionals and businesses. "Recognize that talent is at least as selective as you are and that people who read your job post are asking themselves: "would this be a good client to work with?""

I can effortlessly connect people to my office. There are countless ways to feed my indulgence. Using subcontractors in 2012 is way easier than it was years ago. That's because I can hire anyone, anywhere as long as they have an internet connection. And then I can use very inexpensive technology tools to get them connected to my office. Geography is no longer a limiting factor.

I promote (and teach) entrepreneurship. Some people look down their noses at us outsourceaholics. But contrary to what they may think, my subcontractors like outsourcing with me and do this of their own free will. They are not employees because they don't want to be employees. I look for people that are themselves entrepreneurs. They work from home or have very small organizations and they have a niche expertise. Sometimes I work with budding entrepreneurs – people that are out of work and never want to go back to being employed again. I help them with the process of starting their business – invoicing, bookkeeping, time management, etc. I share with them what I've learned as a business owner. For many of my subcontractors I feel as if I'm helping them become better entrepreneurs.

Outsourceaholics like me promote freedom and flexibility. A great majority of contractors I work with are happier than the employees I encounter at clients. That's because they have a different lifestyle. They make their own hours. They work from whatever location suits them. They can hire and fire their clients. Don't get me wrong – there are plenty of downsides too, the most significant being not having a paycheck during slower times. But I'm very hands off with my contractors. I'm not bothered when they work and how they get their job done as long as they get it done on time and they do what they say they're going to do. That's a different experience than you'll have at most employers. For some it's a great change.

As an outsourceaholic, I don't have to explain what I do and especially why I hire and why I fire. don't have to watch what I say. I can ask about a person's family because it's fun to talk about their kids. I can learn about a person's religion because it's interesting to me. For the most part, I don't have to fear being slapped with a discrimination lawsuit. I don't need to have an exit interview or have them sign a waiver of all liability. I don't have to pay severance or fear the same kind of recriminations I have with an employee. If a contractor doesn't do what he or she says they're going to do I can just stop using them in the future. It's as simple as that.

Finally, I can try people out. Hiring an employee is a huge commitment. Sometimes it works, and sometimes it doesn't. Untangling oneself from this relationship can be painful and complicated. Not so with a subcontractor. If things

238

are working then that's great – we'll keep working together. If it's not working then oh well...best of luck elsewhere.

My name is Gene Marks and I am an outsourceaholic. Don't even try to intervene.

How To Make A Big Mac At Home

To me, McDonalds is awesome.

I only go there a few times a year because I'm no longer 17 years old. But when I do eat at McDonalds it's like an event. I make sure I'm alone. I make sure I have plenty of time. And I only order a Big Mac. With fries. And a large Coke. It's a million calories. And I'm sure if I did this every day, like anything in excess, I'd die prematurely. But it's so darn good. I can drop $200 on a fancy dinner or $8 at a McDonalds and I swear I'd enjoy both meals the same.

But McDonalds proved their awesomeness by doing something else. Something that should be watched by any small business owner (particularly one like me who runs a technology business). They produced two amazing videos about their business. You can find them on You Tube.

In one video, the company's director of marketing shows us exactly why a cheeseburger purchased from one of their restaurants does not look as appealing as the cheeseburger we see advertised on TV or in photos. And in the other video, their executive chef shows us how to make a Big Mac at home and even reveals the secret in the secret sauce.

What is this blasphemy? Giving up secrets to the public?

240

Revealing the mysteries that could potentially keep us away from McDonalds? Showing us the dark magic that goes into photographing a cheeseburger or making a Big Mac?

No, it's just transparency. And it's fascinating. And it's fun. And we should pay attention.

We all know that a McDonalds' cheeseburger looks better on TV than in real life. McDonalds knows that we know. So they're not insulting us by pretending otherwise. They're treating their customers with respect. They're admitting that the steam inside the box deflates the size of the burger. They're confessing that a team of stylists prepare a cheeseburger to be photographed and it's not just a burger purchased from a local store. They admit they "retouch" their product by strategically injecting droplets of ketchup and mustard and "enhancing the color" to make sure that the product is shown in its "best possible light."

The same is done in the Big Mac video. I always thought that the "secret" sauce was truly a secret but instead I've learned that it's made up of ingredients found in any supermarket. And I also learned that there's really nothing special to making a Big Mac at home. It's not such a secret. It really is exactly what they've been telling me since I was ten years old watching Saturday morning cartoons. It's two-all-beef-patties-special-sauce-lettuce-cheese-pickles-onions-on-a-sesame-seed-bun. What McDonalds is saying is that if I want a Big Mac I can just do it myself.

Now, I'm not completely naive. I read that fast food companies use flavor "enhancers" in their beef that are not readily available to the typical consumer. And if you notice in the Big Mac video the chef isn't revealing the exact quantities of the spices used. And c'mon...for what a Big Mac costs, is it really worth the time and effort to make one on your own?

But McDonalds is teaching us something important. Let me compare this to an experience a friend of mine recently had when he was purchasing a new server for his business.

My friend spoke to a local technology guy. The tech guy told my friend that buying a new server was a "very complicated thing." There are security and networking and transferring of data and all sorts of other complex issues that would need to be addressed. And who better to solve all of these issues than the him (at $200 per hour)? Of course, getting a new server for your business (or signing up for a managed server in the cloud) is not something that people do every day. And yes, it takes some computer knowledge and expertise of security and networking. But in reality, the knowledge is available. If my friend wanted, he could read up on the process. He could learn himself. He could do the work on his own. It may take him longer. He may make a few mistakes. But it's not black box. He doesn't necessarily need the tech guy. It's just a choice.

And that's the way technology needs to be sold today. The days of technology guys, programmers, database experts and security consultants naming their price and creating a veil over their work are over. Consumers and small businesses are used to downloading apps or signing up for cloud based services on their own. They've come to rely on a user friendly approach to setting up their applications. They expect to get whatever information they need, if they need it, online. They expect to be treated with respect and intelligence and with the assumption that if they wanted to do it themselves they have that option. They expect transparency.

Which is exactly what McDonalds is teaching us.

Just because I saw how I can make a Big Mac at home am I going to do that? No. It's fun to watch and nice to know but when I want a Big Mac I'm happy to pay the four bucks and get it in a restaurant. I feel a little more intelligent about what I'm eating when I'm eating it. But I'm happy to let McDonalds do the work for me. I just want to enjoy the food. I don't want to make it.

And I find many of my clients wanting the same. I've learned that most of them fall into one of three categories. There's the guy who wants to do it all himself. There's the guy who wants me to do it all for him. And there's the guy who would like to do it with me. As a technology provider I must be prepared to address all three of these customers. I can no longer position myself as some genius with all the secrets whose services must be employed as part of the project. I have to have the confidence in myself to lay out all the facts to my clients and reveal, like McDonalds, my secrets. I have to explain where to get the information they would need if they choose to do the work without me. I have to be ready to lend a hand to those that need it. I have to give my clients choice.

I could mow my own lawn, but I use a landscaper. I could do repairs around my house, but I use a handyman. I could make my own Big Mac, but I choose not to. Is this because I'm lazy? Yes. But it's also because I choose to do other things with my time. Today, smart business owners choose how to spend their time profitably. Some feel that futzing with a new server is a good use of their time and maybe that's the case. But many others choose to outsource this work to an expert while they devote their time to selling or collecting or product design.

The important thing is that they're treated with respect by their tech people during the process. They're given the facts. And they're given the opportunity to choose.

6 TV Shows Every Entrepreneur Should Watch

Last weekend my wife and I caught up on the past four episodes of Mad Men that we previously Tivoed. Yes, things started out slow, but as usual we're loving the series.

There are plenty of TV shows I love that do nothing more than make me laugh. The Daily Show, It's Always Sunny in Philadelphia and Modern Family are three that immediately come to mind. But Mad Men is different. It's pretty much the only drama I watch. For years I persuaded myself that by watching Mad Men (which in case you just moved here from North Korea is about a Madison Avenue advertising firm in the 1960's) I was learning more about business. But let's face it: after four seasons of dutifully watching the show I can admit that I haven't learned much about running a business. I have learned, however, that smoking five packs of cigarettes a day, regularly drinking bourbon before 10AM and having an affair with my daughter's elementary school teacher (and 817 other women) may very well get me in trouble. I've also learned not to have a have a sofa in my office. Sofas can be a bad influence in the workplace.

This doesn't mean that there aren't good, quality, educational shows on TV about small business and entrepreneurship. In fact, I can name at least six shows that I regularly watch which teaches me much about running my company and doing a better job.

Your Business. Yes, I'm partial to this show because I've been on it a bunch of times and love the staff. And it's the only show on national television that's fully devoted to helping small business owners grow and succeed. I like that Your Business is not a show dedicated to startups. It's for people, like myself, who are already in business and looking for answers to our every day problems. It's fast paced and fun to watch. And its host, JJ Ramberg (a small business owner herself) knows her stuff. The show's producers frequently like to send JJ on the road where she interviews small business people at conferences or profiles an interesting company (my favorite is the guy who turned his house into a shrine to honor and sell everything related to "A Christmas Story" movie, much to his wife's frustration). JJ then leads a discussion with a couple of experts back in the studio about the segment. I also like the "elevator pitch" where an entrepreneur pitches his/her product/service to those same "experts". The show also features additional segments and tips on its website. It's worth getting up early on a Sunday to watch or, if you're like me, sleep off your hangover and record it. *MSNBC*

Kitchen Nightmares. Give Gordon Ramsay some credit. This is a British guy in America, advising Americans on how to...what? Cook food? A British guy? I love Gordon Ramsay. I love when he drops the f-bomb. I love when he berates other people. My wife loves when he takes off his shirt to change into his chef's gear. And I love his optimism. Doesn't he realize that dopey guy who spent his life savings to buy that stupid Italian restaurant in that empty strip mall is NEVER going to make it a success? Oh well, it still makes for good TV. And Ramsay never gives up. Nor does he disappoint. His temper tantrums are epic. But they're all with good intentions. And emotions aside, this show is not about running a restaurant. It's about running a business. Creating quality products. Marketing. Production. Hard work. And if you watch it long enough you soon get a feel for which

245

business owner will eventually succeed. They're the ones who realize that if they don't hire the right people, fire the bad ones (oftentimes the chef) and manage their finances the right way they'll soon be out of luck. My advice is to not watch the U.S. version of the show, unless you like feeling superior to simple-minded people from Long Island. Watch the older British episodes that are endlessly replayed on BBC America. That way you can feel superior to simple-minded people from Sussex. *Fox and BBC America*

Shark Tank. You realize that this show was copied from the Dragon's Den, another British show? And, like Kitchen Nightmares, Dragon's Den is a much better show than its American counterpart. There's something about a hopeful entrepreneur being humiliated by a guy with an evil British accent that adds more zest to the experience. Nonetheless both shows are an excellent way for the aspiring startup or business owner looking for money to see what it's really like to face a potential investor. Of course this is Hollywood-type entertainment, but the group of "sharks" (like the "dragons") are experienced investors who, despite their lame arguments and manufactured bickering do wind up asking pertinent questions that any potential investor or banker will ask. Whether we're a startup or have been in business for a while, it's still all about the exit plan. How will our company, which is only just an asset, maximize its value? What is the return on investment? Who is our competition? Can't Mark Cuban just give me a million and we'll call it a day? Forget about all those "how to" books – this show is a fun way to understand the real questions we should all be asking ourselves about our businesses, whether we're looking for financing or not. *ABC*

Flipping Out. Jeff Lewis is a crazy, compulsive, manic, obsessive, micro-manager. In other words, a typical small business owner. He's also a design-savant, specializing in turning his clients' down-market homes that look almost as dumpy as...well...my home and turning them into attractive, hip, sleek dwellings that are instantly re-sellable (or flippable). I interviewed Jeff a few weeks ago and learned that he counts his money in his bathtub. But look, this is America in 2012. Who reads anymore, right? And who actually still takes baths? Just turn on the TV and watch him in action. Like many of us, Jeff runs a small business. And like many of us he struggles getting the most out of his seven people, pleasing his customers, balancing his books, arguing with suppliers and generally trying not to kill himself in the process. My favorite is Zoila the housekeeper. Jeff's mistakes are our learning experiences. *Bravo*

Clark Howard. I'm not going to lie – I've never actually made the time to sit down and watch Clark Howard's CNN show. I don't go out of my way to Tivo it either. But for some reason I keep stumbling upon it, mostly in airport lounges. And I love it. Howard's show is primarily about personal finance and saving money. But it's his personality that endears me. He's not arrogant or preachy. He's a nerd and a nebish...like me. And his advice on personal finance is very relevant to what every small business owner should know. He talks about new technology, how to save money on travel, putting money away for your kids' college education (thank God my kids aren't smart enough to go to an expensive college) and specific tips for saving as a small business owner. You'll feel like you're cheating off that smart kid in science class all over again. But this time it's OK. *HLN*

How I Made My Millions. CNBC does amazing specials about companies and industries that are worth the time of anyone running their own small business. My all time favorite is Cruise Inc: Big Money On The High Seas because what guy hasn't spent at least half a day while on that Royal Caribbean ship trying to figure out how much money that boat is generating? Am I right here guys? Ignore anything that comes on before 8PM, unless you can stay awake watching reports from Wall Street or don't mind being emasculated by Suze Orman. And watch How I Made My Millions which is all about those successful companies that we all know (and many that we don't) and how they came to be. Jelly Belly. Nerf. Herr's Potato Chips. The Marks Group (just kidding... not there yet). Getting advice from so called experts like me is one thing. Watching real life stories about entrepreneurs that succeeded in a big way is...priceless. *CNBC*

A final word - don't laugh when I also recommend **Donald Trump's The Apprentice** or even **Undercover Boss**. OK, you can laugh. But both shows teach a little, just a little, about teamwork, employee management and productivity. I didn't include either on the list above because, well, after a little time watching I'm usually drawn back into Paddy's Pub to hang out with the gang instead.

Technology Trends That You Must Follow

To Stay Competitive

Lessons in IT from Howard Stern

I've listened to The Howard Stern Show on Sirius XM Radio for years. Howard Stern knows how to deliver an entertaining and interesting radio show. But I never thought he would teach me, a small business owner, something about technology projects. Here's how he did.

I recently traded in my beloved Jeep Wrangler for a great Nissan Murano. Unfortunately, the car didn't come with a satellite radio that would let me listen to my beloved Stern show. No problem, I thought. I found a nice Kenwood 6632:JP "satellite ready" radio at Best Buy for only $129.99. I'd be listening to Sal and Richard's prank phone calls in no time!

The next day, I visited a Best Buy store and spoke with Tim in the radio installation area. He said he could install the radio in less than 90 minutes—but he didn't have all the parts. So he wrote out a list of instructions for me and sent me on my way.

Off I went to another Best Buy to purchase a Sirius SCC1 Connect Vehicle Tuner ($59.95) because Tim's store was out of stock. Then, from home, I visited Onlinecarstereo.com, to get the essential Metra Electronics Part #99-746, otherwise known as the Install Kit for my Nissan Murano. That cost another $22.99, plus shipping.

Phew! Howard, I'm almost there.

With all parts now in hand, I set one of the next available appointments with Tim. But when I arrived, I learned I needed yet another part, the Kenwood KCA-SR50 Sirius Interface Box, for $40.99, and—you guessed it—they didn't have it in stock, either. Tim asked one of his techs to pick it up on his way into the store. He told me the guy was only 20 minutes away and it would be no big deal. I agreed, packed up, and settled down for the morning at a nearby Starbucks.

Two hours passed. Tim's tech guy had gotten "held up." It took another hour for him to arrive and for Tim to get going on the installation—which set me back another $191.34. Sirius, not content with its monthly fee, got in on the action by billing me an additional $15 "transfer fee" to switch from my old unit. So, by the time I was back on the road, listening to Robin's news, my $129.99 Sirius radio cost more like $460.26 and at least five hours of my time.

But, hey, I love The Howard Stern Show. And in the end, the experience taught or reminded me of some valuable lessons about getting tech projects done.

Materials on a technology project will almost always cost more than what I'm originally quoted.

When someone selling me software says the price is going to be $5,000, I now know it's going to cost more. Software vendors sometimes "forget" those little add-on modules or third-party tools that make their software actually do close to what they promised it would do. And, just as the Kenwood KCA-SR50 Sirius Interface Box cost about a third of what the actual Kenwood radio costs, those additional items can bump up the cost of a software or hardware purchase by 30% or more.

People will always take more time than promised to complete IT projects.

Tim was very good. But he didn't know that his tech guy got into a fight with his girlfriend that morning, which is why he was late and we had to wait. And Tim's not perfect. He does dozens of car radio installations each week. He can't remember everything he told to every customer and sometimes he forgets a part, like the KCA-SR50 Sirius Interface Box. So more time, and expense, is incurred. He originally told me that the whole installation would take about 90 minutes. The actual time was several more hours. For a technology project, that's about par for the course.

To get a project done right, I need to be significantly involved.

My internal technology projects generally do not succeed unless I'm involved. It's not that I'm some kind of tech genius. But, because this is affecting my business, I need to get intimately familiar with the software (or in this case the parts needed). I need to understand what the techs are doing. I need to stick around in case I'm needed to approve any changes or be told that a tech had a fight with his girlfriend and would be late.

It's incredible that after 20-plus years in technology I can still suffer like this. Then again, I could have researched this better. There's plenty of documentation from Sirius, Best Buy, and consultants that would have explained the process for me well in advance. I could've saved a trip to the store and bought what I needed beforehand from the comfort of my own home. I could have picked up the phone and pushed Tim, no matter how "busy" or reluctant he may have been, to walk me through the process beforehand. And rather than drink coffee that morning, I could have had a shot or two of Jack Daniels. That would have helped, too.

All's well that ends well. The Sirius radio is great. Howard's yelling at Sal again. And this tech project, like all my tech projects, came in three times the cost and three times the effort. No surprises here. And to think, I learned it all from Howard Stern.

Confessions of a (Former) IT Scoundrel

Thinking of doing business with my company? You should proceed with caution. I've made mistakes, and some of my clients have suffered because of them.

My 10-person firm sells popular business software and then provides services such as consulting, training, support, and customizations. We have more than 500 clients. Most are happy, but some are not. The unhappy ones are not to blame. Their dissatisfaction is almost always my fault. In the effort to get a sale, and sometimes long after the sale, I've made errors in judgment. I didn't take the high road when I should have. I took the easy way out. I'm pretty sure that other information technology professionals have done the same. But this is about me, not them.

Am I kidding here? No. To prove it, here are a few real-life examples, with names changed, of how I messed up and failed my clients. I've tried to learn from these mistakes, and you should be on the lookout for warning signs such as these before you give the green light to any IT project.

1. I sold cars to unlicensed drivers.

To this day, I'm amazed by the number of people who will spend a ton of money on software for their entire business after a single demonstration. I spend more time picking out a pair of sneakers than some clients have spent evaluating a business application.

Barr Landscaping turned to my firm to put in a help-desk

system so they could track service issues from the time a ticket is opened to the completion of a customer survey. After one demonstration of our product, Alan Barr, the owner, gave me a thumbs-up and said enthusiastically: "This looks great. Let's get started!" Buying new software should require product research, multiple demos, on-site testing, reference checking, and planning. None of which he had done.

Knowing this, did I take the high road and refuse to move forward? Nope. I said "Super," arguing to myself that he's going to buy from someone, so it may as well be me. I kept my fingers crossed. I took his money. I hoped for the best. And I made him sign paperwork releasing my firm from any liability. Not surprisingly, the software wasn't exactly right and he had to spend a lot more to customize it. We no longer work together.

Have you done all your homework before buying technology? I've learned now to ask questions.

2. I've sent boys to do a man's job.

Need IT training or support? I've learned the hard way about assigning the right person to the job.

We didn't do that for AVM Manufacturing. They purchased a customer relationship management (CRM) product. AVM is a small company with a small budget. Like many IT firms, my company is also small, and my resources are limited. I have experienced people who are certified in the products we sell. I also have people who aren't. I'd like to send my most qualified people out all the time, but if we're busy, that isn't always possible. And clients can be impatient. So the big, important, profitable jobs get our best first.

And AVM? Well, they didn't. I had a bad feeling as I knowingly sent an unqualified person out to perform an installation. My hunch was right. Things took much longer, and my guy almost hosed their entire database. Thank goodness for backups. We got fired. I learned my lesson here, too.

3. I hoped that a Little Leaguer could strike out A-Rod.

Mildred is a nice bookkeeper who a few years ago celebrated her 60th birthday. Unfortunately, she almost didn't make it to 61. At the time, she was put in charge of her company's accounting software upgrade. They might as well have made her manager of the New York Yankees. Nice lady, but wrong skill set.

Yet the owner of the company insisted. I knew she was ill-suited for the job, but I didn't argue further. I kept my mouth shut. I just wanted to sell them the software. As expected, putting Mildred in charge was not a good choice. The project went badly. And here's the thing: The client wound up spending way more money on our services than planned, just to cover Mildred's inexperience.

By not drawing a line in the sand and insisting on a more qualified employee to work with, I failed that client, too. Want your project to be successful? Make sure you've got the right person on the mound. Having learned my lesson, I'll do my best to warn you if he's not.

4. I'd rarely commit.

I dated my wife for seven years before she finally proposed. That's right. She proposed. And it wasn't exactly a proposal, either. She told me to you-know-what or get off the you-know-what. I used to conduct myself the same way with clients.

They would ask me to commit to a fee, and I'd hem and haw. I'd whine that there are too many variables, too many question marks. At best, I'd give a wide estimate ("Gee, that should take between 50 and 892 hours"). Maybe this was because I had been burned many times before by unexpected complications beyond my control.

I've come to realize that I was doing my clients a big disservice by refusing to commit to a fixed price on projects. How could a client have confidence in me if I didn't have the confidence in me? This nagged at me. Just like my wife. Now I've learned to make commitments. I give firm estimates. I put my skin in the game.

5. I said yes too quickly.

John, a manager at an engineering consulting firm, asked me early in the process of reviewing a CRM application if the software "synchronizes with my Smartphone contacts." I said, "Of course." He was happy with my response. I was happy that he was happy.

As it turned out, the software did sync this contact info— only not the contact info he was talking about. He had created certain user fields that were very important to him, and they did not transfer over. Needless to say, John was not happy. I, therefore, was not happy.

John's not an expert at CRM software. I was supposed to be the expert. I was supposed to dig deep, ask the tough questions, get the details. In the heat of trying to get the sale, I didn't really dig deep enough. Important stuff was glossed over. I naively assumed too much and brushed aside important questions. And by doing this, I failed John. We no longer work together.

Now when clients ask about features and functionality, I try my best to show, show, show. I've learned that I can't read people's minds. And saying yes all the time can build unrealistic expectations. It all catches up with you in the end.

Are you still, after reading this, interested in buying technology services from a firm like mine? I know I've failed some clients in the past. But I've learned. And at least now you know what questions to ask.

Making Software Demos Productive

Here are a few things, in no particular order, that this small business owner (and die-hard Phillies fan) would rather do than sit through a software demo: Shave my tongue. Travel to North Korea. Watch a cricket match. Root for the Mets.

Unfortunately, I'm forced to sit through more software demonstrations than the average guy. That's because I'm in the tech business. I sell business software to small companies. If our technology isn't a good fit, clients often hire us to help them find something else. Here's what I think about most of the demos I've seen from software vendors: They suck. They're often a big waste of time.

Don't these guys get it? Enough with the Microsoft PowerPoint presentations, the technospeak, the pointing and clicking and shuffling. Enough with the chitchat, the bad jokes, laptops that freeze up, and blurry projectors. I realize that some of this stuff is unavoidable. But please—let's keep it to a minimum. Just give me the bottom line. Show me how your software will solve my problem. MY problem. Not some fake company called "Adventure Land Industries" that sells playground equipment and fertilizer.

But you don't have to simply endure software demos. You can take control. You can even make them productive. Here are a few ways how:

Make the vendor do two demos. The first is a "tell me" demo. That's their chance to sing, dance, spit fire, and regale you with stories of just how superwonderful their product is.

257

When that propaganda is done, you schedule a second session. This is called the "show me" demo. It's the real demo. Supply the vendor with your data. Give the vendor a few of your scenarios (such as placing an order, recording a sale, etc.) and then say, "Show me." Don't believe it until you see it.

Have an agenda. Agree on what you're going to discuss in advance. I don't like being in a car when someone else is driving. I need possession of the remote control at all times. And I don't like being in meetings where people I hardly know—especially software vendors—tell me when I can get up and go. Make sure the vendor focuses on the 20% to 30% of the app that you'll actually need, and not the fluff (like "advanced order processing" and "digital dashboard alerting processes").

Agree on a stop time. The vendor should be able to show you what you need in 90 minutes. And have your office manager call your cell phone when the agreed time approaches so you can make a graceful exit if the vendor is still rattling on.

Minimize on-site demos with their time-consuming hellos, goodbyes, and drivel about soccer games and vacations (do we have to learn all about the salesperson's life details, too)? It's 2010, and there's something called the Internet. Most of this stuff can be done online, without having to host some software vendor and his suitcase full of matrimonial complaints. Bring the guy on-site when you're much further along in the process.

Ask about pricing up front. A common trait among vendors is that they try to leave the pricing of their products to the very last minute. It's like some closing trick they picked up at a cheesy sales seminar. Don't fall for it. Start the demo by asking how much. You'll know the salesman is lying if he says, "Oh, I need to check on that." Trust me. He knows what it all costs. And we know it's overpriced, too. So let's just save everyone some time here and determine right off the bat whether this software is even in the ballpark. Leave the negotiations to later. But make sure to act shocked ("Excuse me, sir?") when you hear the initial price so the vendor knows that a discount request is surely in the cards.

Focus on the output. No matter what the software vendors tell you, no matter what features, colors, language, pop-ups, pinups, or push-ups they demonstrate, never forget that what you're getting is just a big old database. In the end, you're going to need data from that database—be it in a report, an invoice, a packing slip, a layoff notice. So zero in on the output. When you have the "show me" demo, make sure you're shown how all of this will look. And find out what's involved if the output isn't to your liking. It's easy to customize? Really? Well, here's my invoice. Go ahead and customize it. Now. While I watch.

Ask the vendor about the competition. This is not forbidden. The competition is out there, and if the vendor knows what he's doing then he better well know what his competition is doing. What makes his product better than theirs? Ask him to rattle off five benefits of choosing his application over someone else's. Ask him to compare pricing and talk about features. And if your vendor starts bashing another vendor, guess what? Maybe that's not such a bad thing. Maybe your vendor loves his product so much that he's offended that you would even be considering an alternative. I like that kind of passion!

Don't be nice. Crashes should be unacceptable. Lack of demo data is embarrassing. Blaming the computer when things go wrong is a no-no. Your gut may be right—if the software doesn't work well in a demo environment, exactly how is it going to work in real life? There may be good reasons when something goes wrong during a demo. Ask. You'll have plenty of time to get answers during that awkward pause while the vendor's computer is rebooting.

Maybe I'm being just a little too harsh on the software

vendors. But these are ways to minimize the pain and make the sessions more productive. And maybe sitting through a demo really isn't that bad—hey, it couldn't be worse than watching the Mets play.

Advice for Brides
and Business Owners

When I was about to get married twenty years ago my dad said to me "Son... getting married will be the last decision you'll ever make." Boy, was he right.

Marriage is a long term decision. Just like buying technology.

For example, Apple Corporation's a great company. With smart people. And even they've had their headaches choosing the right technology partner. Their communications service partner, AT&T, has suffered connection glitches in certain parts of the country. The guys who manufacture their iPhones have antenna issues. And now their primary resource for supplying iPad monitors are having supply problems.

Those guys at Apple may be smart. But they clearly need some help choosing the right partner. My advice? They should watch a couple of episodes of Bridezillas.

C'mon, you know the show. Big, hairy brides-to-be yell and scream at their wedding planners, threaten their own bridesmaids, throw tantrums during photo shoots and have spectacular meltdowns just minutes before walking down the aisle . And all for the sake of having that perfect wedding. Which never really happens in real life.

These brides don't get it. It's not about the wedding. It's about the marriage...and who they're marrying. Apple execs have found this out. But, unfortunately, a lot of small business owners don't get this. Especially when it's time to make big purchases of technology for their companies.

It's not about the technology. And it's not about the wedding. It's about the partner. And the long term relationship you're about to enter.

Because the technology industry is changing for small companies like mine. Microsoft doesn't just want your Windows business. They want your database, security and network management business too. And Sage doesn't want you just to purchase their ERP software. They want you to buy their CRM software too. IBM's software is meshed with its hardware. Dell doesn't just sell computers. They sell printers and monitors and storage components and networking devices. All of these companies tell you that you'll be better off sticking with their products. They don't just want customers. They want customers for life. You're not buying technology anymore. You're entering into a marriage. And you don't want to wake up to find yourself married to Mel Gibson one day, now do you?

Once you implement your new accounting software, or go live with that Customer Relationship Management system, or turn the switch on that upgraded network the honeymoon is over. You're going to be in bed with that vendor for the long term. So choose wisely.

When choosing, smart penny pinchersI know start with their vendors' financial history. They request credit reports from services like Dun and Bradstreet and Hoovers. If public, they research the company's recent SEC filings. If private they ask for financial data. They want to know how profitable these companies are. How many employees they have. How long they've been in business. What kind of cars their executives drive. If you're going to rely on someone else's software to run your entire business, you want to make damn sure that that company's going to be in business over the long term in case you're having any problems. This goes ten-fold if you decide to host your data with a third party. What happens if they suddenly close up shop? Where's your data? How can you get support?

Referrals are important too. But not those spoon fed referrals from the technology vendor. The best referrals are the ones you get yourself. Go to monster.com or careerbuilder. com and search for the technology you're considering. If you see a company advertising a job where that software or expertise is a part of the requirements they're looking for then that's a good indication that they own the technology you're about to buy. Call them and ask about their experience with the vendor. What happened after the sale? Do they pick up the phone when there's a problem? Are their support people knowledgeable? Do they update their technology frequently? Do they care if the floral arrangements lack yellow roses? Are they pro-active? Guys - what would you do if you saw your fiancée scream at her family, kick over tables and punch holes in the drywall just days before your wedding? Same as me.

Nothing. Let's not make the mistake when buying technology for our businesses. Many of those wonderful girls on Bridezillas make the mistake of visiting the catering hall where the wedding is going to happen. Good idea…but wrong place. They should be visiting the trailer park where they'll be living once the affair is over. Many business owners make the same mistake when buying technology. They rely too much on what their vendor is telling them. And not enough on their own eyes.

If you're going to spend a big chunk of change on a new business management system, you should visit the vendor beforehand. Do their offices look like George Clooney? Or Zach Galifianakis? To find this out, some clients of mine have sent key people to end-user training at the vendor's location before they even purchase the technology. Why not? They spend a few days with users from other companies. They get

263

to speak to the vendor's trainers and support people and NOT the sales guys. They can get a sense of the company's culture and attitude towards their existing customers. A typical end user training may cost a few thousand dollars. But if you're about to spend six figures on a brand new business system you may find this little investment well worth the money.

Smart business owners I know have looked to purchase technology from companies that have strong partner channels too. That's not to say that some companies provide good long term support completely from their headquarters. But large companies like HP, Microsoft and Cisco have found that building a strong network of partners helps them service their smaller customers more efficiently. We need to make sure these partners hold the right certifications, are well staffed and can refer us to some of their own customers so we can determine if they do good, reliable work. We want to try calling them at all hours of the night with questions just to see how responsive they are. We want to ask how long these partners have been affiliated with their technology vendors and try to gauge how happy or frustrated they may be with their relationship. This could be a pretty good indicator of our own long term happiness with the vendor too.

And in the end, we also want to be good partner. God knows, no marriage is perfect – just ask Jon and Kate. And no technology is perfect either. Instead of throwing a hissy fit like a typical Bridezilla, Apple has worked with its partners to solve those inevitable problems when they occur. For a small business owner, the technology will never work completely well all the time. But if we have a good partnership with our vendors, and don't behave like a Bridezilla, we too can overcome whatever problems we'll ultimately encounter. With no hissy fits.

Is The Cloud Ready For Small Business?

The summer of 2012 was not a good one for The Cloud.

The big news was that Twitter had suffered its second major outage in the past five weeks. Two Amazon outages over the past month "certainly got everyone's attention." It was reported that "...one, in late June, was sparked by a violent thunderstorm which cut power, setting up a chain of events that put many Amazon customers offline for hours. That came just two weeks after another significant outage in the same U.S. East data center." A violent thunderstorm? Not even a tornado or an earthquake? C'mon Amazon...you've got to come up with a better reason than that.

It's easy to pick on Twitter and Amazon. But they're not the only ones letting us down. Hundreds of thousands of sales and service people were left in the cold when Salesforce.com went blank . A Google Talk outage hit a "majority of users." Microsoft's Windows Azure cloud went down in Europe. Few details were made available at the time, but Microsoft says it was "on the case" which I'm sure brought relief to so many of their customers while waiting for their applications to come back online. And the UK government, on the eve of the Olympics, reported issues affecting its flagship CloudStore service which only affected the ability of their suppliers to process orders and get paid.

Does this all concern you? As a small business owner,

it should. I can understand these problems happening a few years ago. I could be more patient if this were a less mature technology or a technology that's not constantly being jammed down my throat as the solution to all of my technology problems. But apparently it's not. Because even some of our largest companies can't seem to get it together. Small businesses don't want to hear about 99% uptime, particularly when that 1% downtime coincidentally just happens to occur when we're trying to get an invoice out the door.

I am writing this from a café in London where' I'm travelling. I'm using Microsoft Word except it's not installed on my HP mini-laptop. I'm using Word on a server that is hosted somewhere in Pennsylvania (I think). That's because, for over a year now, my entire company has hosted Microsoft Word through a cloud workspace provider. And not just Word. They host all of our applications – Microsoft Office, Exchange, QuickBooks, our customer relationship management application, our company databases and all of our files. This company is doing a good job but they're no Amazon or Microsoft. Should I be nervous?

My business is completely reliant on our hosted cloud provider. I have ten people and they are all accessing my server. Our entire accounting system is there. We do all of our invoicing and payments on the cloud. Our scheduling, job history, project information, billing data, quotes, forecasts, payroll, contracts, even my phone system….they're all hosted by someone else. I am drinking the cloud Kool-Aid and I'm starting to get the feeling that the guy who told me to drink it wasn't exactly looking after my best interests.

Small businesses like mine are targeted as those best suited to benefit from the power of The Cloud. Not a day seems to go by without news of another new and hot company of twelve year olds who are receiving millions of dollars from

266

VC firms or launching their ground-breaking and spectacular cloud application to the world. Salesforce.com, Microsoft, Sage and dozens of other fine CRM providers promote their applications to small business. Freshbooks leads an industry of developers who want us to do our time and billing with them. The online project management industry, led by companies like Basecamp, promotes their inexpensive ways to manage our critical accounts online. We're told it's less expensive (at least in the short term, although if you add up the monthly cost of many of these applications and extrapolate them over their lives the cost can be much more). They're easy to setup. They're perfect for companies like mine, with no offices and people spread out geographically. There's no IT muss and fuss. Everyone's doing it.

Except everyone's not doing The Cloud. My company serves over 600 clients and, unlike me, less than a third of them are reliant on The Cloud for their mission critical applications. My clients in the healthcare and financial services industries avoid The Cloud like The Plague. Their systems are still in-house and locked down. Do these people know something that the rest of us don't? Yes they do. For them, The Cloud is not yet ready for prime time.

If The Cloud was ready for primetime, services like Twitter, Amazon's EC2, Salesforce.com, Google Talk and Microsoft Azure wouldn't go down. Ever. But they do. And companies suffer. Particularly those companies that rely on these services for their own mission critical objectives.

Twitter may be fun for most, but there are a growing number of companies that rely heavily on the service for advertising, information and communication. For example, the folks at Netflix, Pinterest and Instagram I'm sure weren't too pleased when EC2 went down. Without EC2, they (and so many others who host their web based commerce information with Amazon) watched helplessly as their own businesses inexplicably dropped. Not a good feeling. I personally know many business users of Google Talk who rely on the chat application for conducting conferences with their clients. Companies in Europe who save their files on Microsoft's Skydrive or rely on Microsoft Office 365 online services were out of luck. And if you were trying to provide service or sales follow-ups to your customers and prospects using your Salesforce.com application you were stuck.

And let's face it everyone, even when these services are up and running there are still headaches. The London coffee shop where I'm writing this has "free Wi-Fi" but the performance is terrible and it's taking me twice as long to write this as it would if I were on my normal desktop. Could it be the Olympics going on a few miles away? No, because I frequently suffer the same issue in Cleveland hotels and Las Vegas conference centers. Sometimes I'm faced with a technical challenge with a Google Doc or an e-mail error message and hit a technical support wall. Do these people have phones anymore? And there have been at least 10 times over the past year alone where my cloud computing service has hiccupped…throwing me offline or being inaccessible for anywhere between five minutes and an hour. All with good reasons. But it's still not very comforting.

This is the state of The Cloud in 2012. And it will continue into 2014. And I endure.

The tech guys tell us to make sure we're backing up our data and to be wary of security. Like that solves the problem. But it really doesn't. I do backup our company data (ironically using other cloud based backup services like Carbonite) so I'm not really worried about losing any information. And I'm not that worried about security either (and maybe that's just naïve). I feel like the cloud companies who host my information are putting more secure measure in place than I ever did when I had everything on my own server. I think most small business owners would agree with this.

It's just that big, reliable cloud services are still going down too often. And big companies, with big IT staffs and big budgets, are suffering. And to small business owners, already nervous about this new technology, these events do not give us a warm and cozy feeling. Yes we see the potential. And we're romanced by the opportunities. But is the cloud really ready for us? Or should we give it more time to mature. There's no definitive answer. But one thing's for sure: there are still a lot of unanswered questions. I'm enjoying our cloud based service. But that doesn't mean I'm not keeping my fingers crossed every day. And if in 2013 and 2014 you're considering the cloud for your mission critical business applications that might not be a good thing for now.

Haven't Adopted Mobile Technology For Your Business? Good For You!

Your business needs a mobile app! The world is going mobile! Don't get left behind! Does this sound familiar? It does to me. I hear these warnings all the time.

And everyday I see more evidence of the mobile "explosion." I'm told that the number of cellphones in this country now exceeds our population and that Apple shipped 17 million iPads in the last quarter alone. I read the reports about how tablet sales are predicted to soon outstrip sales of PCs. Like everyone else I'm amazed by these numbers. Yes, we're living in an increasingly mobile world. I've got a smart phone. You've got a smart phone. Our employees all have smart phones. And we all love our smart phones. We get it.

Except in our businesses. Because there...we're not really getting it, are we?

Why aren't our businesses making better use of mobile technology? Sure, you may have purchased smart phones for your people so they can talk or text on behalf of your company. But don't you feel that these devices are significantly underused? Doesn't it seem like there's a lot more you can be doing with mobile technology to make your people more productive? I feel that way. So, are we missing something? Well, you're not. My company serves over 600 clients. We sell them customer relationship management applications. There are mobile solutions available that work with the applications we sell. But here's what I'm seeing: none of my clients are truly using mobile technology very well. So don't worry... you're not alone.

And don't feel bad. You are not in the wrong either. Like me, and my clients, you probably have not truly adopted mobile technology for many good reasons.

You haven't adopted this kind of technology because you probably haven't decided on its objectives. It's not about phone calls or Angry Birds or email. It's about data entry and data retrieval. Imagine a clip board or an order book without a pencil. It's about instant updating of your back end systems from wherever the data is entered. It's about speeding up the time it takes to get an order processed, inventory bought and payment collected. It's about scheduling service, completing tasks and doing paperwork without the paper and without having to come back into the office. There are many ways to use mobile technology. But, like me, you probably haven't decided where yet. If you don't know the objectives of a technology then stop right there.

And you may not have agreed on which of your people are most suitable for a mobile solution. It could be about giving that guy in your truck at a customer's house a way to easily fill out a work-order and schedule a delivery. Or a sales associate on your shop floor who needs to ring up a sale on aisle five, swipe a credit card while updating your accounting system and automatically adding that customer to your mailing list for future sales offers. Or if you've got people in your warehouse then they might be able to use a mobile device to count inventory and update materials movement immediately back to your system.   Maybe you've got professionals at clients who want to check on a recent filing or an upcoming schedule. Or you've got sales reps who need to look up pricing or place an order. Or maybe you don't have any of these scenarios and don't need mobile technology at all!

Another reason why you're not using mobile technology in your business: there aren't a lot of pickings to choose from. Sure, there are task managers and calendars and reminder apps that you can download for free from iTunes. But have you encountered many (or any?) enterprise level applications that will accomplish the tasks I've mentioned above quickly, inexpensively and are easy to implement? Probably not. So it's not you. It's the software community. They're just getting started. A few vendors have already created some of these apps. But they're still not very good yet. And you will have to be patient. Because these mobile applications will mature. The big makers, like Microsoft, Sage, Oracle, Epicor, SAP and NetSuite will get better and better at making more affordable applications that will enter orders, update inventory, do quotes...all that stuff. From the field or from your warehouse. And then integrate with their back end systems. It will come. But we're not there yet. Which is why you're not there yet. My advice here is if you like your software vendor, then stick with them and rely on them for your mobile solutions. That's what they do.

And let's also admit that the infrastructure isn't there yet either. Unfortunately, that's another obstacle you're facing, right? Like those days of yore when Microsoft would make software that required more and more hardware to run, today's software developers are making mobile apps that increasingly rely on accessing and downloading data in the field from your back end systems or cloud based data sources. These apps must rely on your wireless carrier's capabilities. And we all know what that means: dropped connections, loss of service, dead zones and other inconsistencies that hinder true mobile usage. The sad fact is that our country's infrastructure for conducting business in the cloud is still very immature. Things will get better. But in the meantime salesmen, service techs and others

272

in the field are still bashfully asking their customers if they can "use their phones to call in this order" because they can't link up to the office. It happens all the time.

You may be confusing "mobile" with "smart phones." iPhones and Droids are great little devices for communicating and playing games. They are useful for getting directions, looking up a phone number and checking emails. But they will never be much more than that for a business. Your people cannot use these devices for data input for very long without contracting arthritis and slowly going blind.

The right devices for mobile technology are tablets. And the tablet industry is growing fast...but still relatively young. Businesses are trying to figure out the right tablet for... business. Right now most tablets are for consumers. The iPad is an amazing device, but it's expensive and very locked down. Creating a mobile strategy around iPads means potentially limiting yourself to available apps from the Apple community that may not be as flexible for your needs. Although lagging significantly behind iPad sales, Android based tablets like the Samsung Galaxy may be a better solution for your mobile strategy. Besides being significantly cheaper, Google's operating system is much more open than Apple's so you can develop more customized applications for your business. And of course you get much better integration with Google's apps like Gmail and Google Docs. But with this openness comes a cost: security. And what about Microsoft's new Surface tablet which is expected to hit the market this year? Besides being priced comparably with Android based tablets, Microsoft tells us it will run Windows 8, work well with Office applications, come with a built in keyboard and be ready for their huge partner community to use as a basis for developing business applications. That sounds pretty good. But then again, it's Microsoft....

So you haven't yet adopted mobile technology for your business. Good for you. You're prudent and careful. You don't invest in something that's not yet proven. You have better things to spend your money on. But you're keeping a close watch on this, right? I hope so. I am. Because mobile technology will mature. The applications will get better. The infrastructure will catch up. The devices will become cheaper and faster. And, within a few years, we will all hopefully be able to do things much quicker and better from just about anywhere.

Why Google Is About To Make Us Laugh

"I was watching Animal Planet and did you know that the male seahorse has the baby? And I was thinking, "Why don't they just call that the female seahorse?"

That line was from Jim Gaffigan. I wrote about him earlier. Last year he released his newest performance to the public, called Mr. Universe. But it's not a typical release. There's no DVD. It's all online.

Years ago comedians didn't have these choices. The big names, like Bob Newhart, Bill Cosby and Redd Foxx would have their performances recorded, mixed and sold as records. Or cassette or 8-track tapes. Although TV helped comedians reach a wider audience, the bread and butter of their earnings still came from their concert performances and record sales. Even as the technology changed, the products were still pretty much the same: records and tapes turned into videos which turned into DVDs. All made by production companies who then paid the performer a royalty.

But recently, technology taken a huge jump forward. A jump that affects not only comedians like Jim Gaffigan, but anyone who produces content that they want to mass deliver to a large audience. For many of us, this is intimidating. We don't want to miss the boat. Gaffigan is by no means a technology guy. He spends his time thinking up things like "why doesn't every fortune cookie say 'you're about to eat a stale cookie?'"

275

And Gaffigan, like most comedians, does not consider himself to be a business person either. Like many entrepreneurs, he has little desire to be rich and famous. All he wants to do is create great content and deliver that content to as many people as possible who enjoy it. He's unable to do this for free, so of course he's going to try and earn the best living that he can doing it. To accomplish this he must create a business. And he has to use technology. So he has. And he does.

Enter Google+ Hangouts. More particularly what they call Hangouts "On Air."

For those of you not familiar with Google+ it's Google's own social networking community which competes (and currently struggles) against Facebook. The company's intention is to entice many of its hundreds of zillions of daily visitors away from Facebook into Google's community. Social media pundit Chris Brogan thinks the platform will ultimately be a hit, saying recently: " I'm nuts about Google+. (It's) the next big thing. (And I don't make such predictions lightly.) Why? The platform is more than just a boon for networking and marketing--you can also put it to work to boost your revenues, online and off."

A big part of Google + is Google + Hangouts, which is nothing more than their video chat service. Nothing more... for now. For now, up to nine users can chat with each other like Skype or iChat. But that's about to change. In a big way. With Hangouts On Air. Chee Chew hinted at bigger plans. And these plans will affect entrepreneurs like Jim Gaffigan.

"There is the vegetarian Hot Pocket for those of us who don't want to eat meat, but would still like diarrhea."

Think that's funny? I think it's hilarious! And today I can get more of it.

That's because today I can take advantage of the newest innovation for distributing content: I'll be able to download or stream new material from one of my favorite comedians. That's what Gaffigan is doing. Following in the footsteps of successful releases by other comedians like Louis CK and Aziz Ansari, Gaffigan's 993,000 Twitter followers and anyone else can pay just five bucks to download his latest offering and watch it whenever and wherever they want. At a third of the cost of the CDs he's betting that even more of his fans will prefer to watch him say things like "I come from a very big family... nine parents".

And make no mistake...it's a big bet. Gaffigan told me that he's invested around a quarter of a million bucks to make this video. Of his own money. He paid for his own production team. He hired public relations people and social media marketing experts to assist him in getting the word out. He hired consultants and developers to create a download process that's easy as possible because that's what everyone has told him to do: make it as easy as possible for a fan to buy his product. And even though the cost is a third of what someone would pay for a DVD and more content is provided, Gaffigan is still very sensitive about providing as much value as possible. He's even giving away a dollar for each purchase to support the Bob Woodruff Foundation.

Will he get his money back? Will fans embrace this new medium? Will he lose his shirt? Should he have done more research? Should he have included bacon? Should he have had a better marketing plan? Will the technology work as promised? Anyone who's introduced a new product has had the same fears. Well, almost. Especially when it's something they've never tried before.

And already, this new method is about to become obsolete. Thanks to Google + Hangouts. Because soon...

Google + will allow it's members to broadcast their content via their Hangouts On Air platform to an unlimited audience... not just nine people. In other words, Google + Hangouts will become everyone's own individualized TV station. Anyone can tune in.

And once again, content providers like Jim Gaffigan are going to have to adjust. Because, like the record albums, cassette tapes and DVDs of yore, the "video download" technology that he's using today will soon be old hat. Corporate trainers, presenters, meeting planners, salespeople, and yes... comedians will be forced to adopt this new technology if they want to keep themselves fresh and stay close to their audiences. Thanks to Hangouts On Air Gaffigan's next product will be different. I predict that he will stream a live show online to his Google+ followers. Using the developer's tools that Chew talks about in the video above, he'll have a programmer create a custom interface for the show. Maybe he'll stream the show for free. Why not? Other than today's streaming technology, it doesn't cost him anything! Maybe he'll sell advertising time. Maybe he'll charge a buck. Maybe he'll simultaneously record the show and make it available for re-streaming for a reasonable fee.

Maybe Gaffigan will cut back his concert schedule too. Instead of just tweeting jokes like "The good news is that I just a jellybean I found on the ground of our apartement. The bad news is it was a tiny ball of Play Doh" or posting little videos of his concert performances he stays at home with his wife and four kids and broadcasts his comedy from the den.

Gaffigan has millions of fans. And, just like today's readers of the news, they all prefer to get his comedy in different ways. I'm no metrics expert, but I have no doubt that the Mr. Universe download that he's making available today will be a success. He will probably sell hundreds of thousands of downloads. But there's no guarantee. A lot of work and money and resources and time and angst went into this. And, like any professional, he will probably feel like he's still not getting his beloved product out to as many people as he would like.

Google is about to change this for him. And for anyone else that's looking to broadcast their content to a large audience.

The Economy, The World...

Your Business

Farting His Way To Profits

I've never had much luck with heroes. Back when I was an adolescent, I worshipped the Fonz. That was until I found out that in real life he was just another skinny Jewish guy—like me. I moved on to idolize Gene Simmons from the rock group KISS, only to reach the same conclusion. My hero worship continued to prove disappointing even as I grew older: Et tu, A-Rod?

But I have good news to report. As a 40-something small-business owner, I think I've found a hero I can keep. His name is Joel Comm. Has he swam the Atlantic Ocean? Saved millions of lives? Discovered a cure for the common cold? Nope. Comm's just making a ton of money selling farts.

His iFart Mobile, a software application that emits the sound of flatulence on an iPhone, became one of the top downloads of all time on Apple's iPhone App Store in December 2008, selling more than 350,000 units at 99¢ a pop in less than one month. This was in the middle of a recession.

Comm's been an entrepreneur all his life. In 1997, he sold a gaming site to Yahoo! that now exists as Yahoo! Games. The company he currently runs, InfoMedia, consists of dozens of websites offering shopping options, free stuff, website reviews, and books he's written. It seems he'll always be thinking up new things to sell. So when Apple launched its App Store, Comm decided to experiment with it as a way to make even more money. The recession didn't enter into his thinking. Why should it? He just did what business owners and entrepreneurs have been doing since the dawn of mankind: he thought of something that would sell, and he decided to…let 'er rip.

I'm no Joel Comm, but we certainly have things in common. At my company, I'm constantly trying to come up with new products to sell, more services to provide, and more ways to serve our clients and create new revenue streams. But contrary to what most would think, neither Comm nor I are doing this just when we're in a recession. We're always doing this. Because when we see a potential need, we try to come up with a way to make money by servicing that need.

No recession is going to stop us from risking a few bucks if we see the opportunity to make a lot more. We're just making different decisions as to where we'll risk our money. The auto and financial services industries recently haven't been looking like great places to risk our capital. Health care, energy, and construction, given the government's spending plans, seem better bets. But these are all just guesses. And, though the choices change with the economic times, the basic return on investment decisions still remain the same. Granted, getting our hands on money during a recession is more challenging. But there are always plenty of good investments to make.

A recession doesn't change the fundamentals of buying low and selling high. Comm created a product with a couple of funny sounds and a few features that an application developer in high school could write. The cost to manufacture was minimal. It had to be. I mean, how much was someone going to pay for a fart, anyway?

Of course, even savvy entrepreneurs like Comm know that making a product is barely half the task. It has to be marketed and distributed. Do these business basics change because a recession is going on? Considering that he sold hundreds of thousands of his sounds in a month, I'm going to take a leap and say no.

I love how, when there's a recession, all the experts start giving us advice on how to run a business. Like keeping overhead low is suddenly a new concept. Of course we know this—just look at the iFart model. It cost little to make and distribute and almost nothing to support. I can guarantee you these same factors would be in place whether Comm sold the iFart in 2008 or 1998.

Recessions come and go. Fortunes go up and down. Governments try to intervene. The media stokes the flames. And through it all, entrepreneurs like Joel Comm and business owners like myself try to carry on.

Startup Tips From Paris Hilton

People often ask me whether now is a good time to start a new business. I think it is. But don't take my word for it. Just ask Paris Hilton. I just love writing about her.

A few years ago Paris was the star and executive producer of an MTV series, "Paris Hilton's My BFF." In it, contestants vied for the privilege of being her best friend by competing against each other in "rigorous challenges that will test their smarts, wit, loyalty, party skills and, perhaps most importantly, their hotness." No. I am not making this up.

Paris and MTV started this venture despite indicators of a recession at that time, and it did well. You can bet that investors sank some serious money into this production, employing script writers, producers, directors, camera guys, makeup artists and pole-dancing specialists. This show had a second season, with lots of "lavish parties, fabulous fashion and plenty of time to impress Paris." Please, please Paris, pick me!

If Paris Hilton is can succeed with this ridiculous venture, doesn't that tell us something? It tells me that anytime can be a really excellent time for anyone, even Paris Hilton, to be an entrepreneur. And here are a few reasons why.

We all know the financing environment hasn't been great. But how terrible can it be if someone saw fit to finance "Paris Hilton's My BFF"?

Maybe not as terrible as we thought. Interest rates were at a historic low. A recent study showed that access to credit is improving for small businesses. The Small Business Administration has started loan programs to boost financing options. Nationally, loan volume has increased. Most banks have cleaned up the worst of their balance sheet messes. Big companies are issuing bonds again.

Loans and investments are being made. To Paris Hilton. And to good companies, with good track records and good management.

And speaking of laying people off, despite however many millions the Labor Department estimates are jobless in this country, statistics show that none of them have any desire to be Paris' BFF. Sure, they don't have the kind of cash to invest that Paris has. Most probably they don't even look as good in a bikini. But they can bring to a startup a lot of other resources: brains, big company knowledge, college educations, real world experience. These people are YOUR potential BFFs … and they're out there looking for you, too.

So where do you find them? Don't worry — you don't have to host your own reality show. There are other, better places to search for talent. Places that were in their infancy or didn't even exist a decade ago. For example, most states are now posting lists of people who have applied for unemployment insurance in order to help them get jobs. websites, both free and for-pay, are teeming with prospective talent. Besides the obvious destinations like Careerbuilder.com, monster.com and Craigslist.com, you can find a bunch of available freelancers on Elance.com, or technical propeller heads on Dice.com.

So there are a lot of good people out there right now to help the startup. And good technologies too. Technologies that bring down the cost of starting and running a small business to far less than the cost of taking Paris out on the town for a night of partying.

For example, startups can rent hosted phone systems, accounting software and technical services for low monthly payments (or in some cases for nothing at all). Shared office space is common. Virtual private networks can be set up on the cheap to create a business in the cloud. Self-service technologies are available to provide customer help round the clock. Smartphones allow us to be connected anywhere all the time. Remote technologies enable us to hire talent anywhere in the world and connect them into our networks. These tools have helped us cut travel costs and time out of the office — allowing us to conduct conference calls for free and online meetings with people all over the world.

Marketing and service tools, like mass e-mail software and social networking sites, allow us to connect to customers and find new markets while sitting in our bathrobes (or in Paris' case, tanning by the pool). Startup companies can produce videos on the cheap and distribute them to a worldwide audience. We can network with investors and potential customers over the Web. We can cut accounting and legal costs by researching free forms and data online. Our startups can look like big companies like never before. That may even help a short, bald guy like me catch Paris' eye, right?

Besides all of this low-cost technology out there for the startup, there's also a huge amount of free and inexpensive resources available. There are nonprofit groups, like the Service Corps of Retired Executives (SCORE) and Small Business Development Centers, who help small businesses with marketing, management and financing issues and don't charge a dime. There are CEO groups like Vistage and EO Network who, for an annual fee, bring together like-minded leaders into groups to hash out problems that start ups face. There are online business communities where budding entrepreneurs can share problems. There are business coaches, training videos and hundreds and hundreds of websites offering free advice, ideas, and consultation to start up businesses.

So is a recession a good time to start a new business? Well, you can ask the founders of Microsoft, Fedex and Burger King, who all started their companies during recessions. Or better yet just ask Paris Hilton. She knows. And besides, she's way hotter.

Recession Lesson 1: How Most Small Businesses Beat the Recession

There are about 20 million small businesses right now in this country, depending on who you ask. And the great majority have survived the Great Recession of 2008-2009. My business is one of them. And as we emerge into recovery, the remaining many will be stronger than ever before. Because Charles will definitely be in charge. And I don't mean Scott Baio. I'm talking about the other Charles.

Darwin.

We're all witnessing natural selection in real life—the kind of selection process that would impress even Simon Cowell. And the business owners who have emerged from this Great Recession have emerged stronger for three big reasons.

The first is happening right before our eyes. It's companies such as Wal-Mart, McDonald's, Best Buy, and Honda becoming healthier at the hands of Linens 'n Things, Applebees, Circuit City, and General Motors. Watch for more natural selection to occur as the economy turns from recession into recovery. Watch how the companies still standing will be standing stronger. The big names will make the news, but many smaller companies, like mine, are seeing the same benefits.

Because, like the competitors of Lehman Brothers, Bear Stearns, and electronics chain Tweeter, the landscape is opening up. There was just too much stuff. Too many companies. Too many stores. And now that the market is adjusting to this reality, the weak are falling. Want to see this happening in real time? Just drive by your local strip mall.

The excesses of our economy are right now cleaning themselves out. And many savvy small businesses are benefiting from this cleansing. Our competitors, newly on the scene, poorly prepared but able to hide these inadequacies during the boom times, are now facing their fatal shortcomings as the downturn deepens, leaving the stronger survivors with the opportunity of more and better work at fairer prices to boot. Like all those unnecessary coffee shops, restaurant chains, and clothing stores at the strip mall, some of our competitors shouldn't have been there in the first place. Good riddance. The ghost of Darwin is chasing these weaker companies into oblivion.

I can see it in my neighborhood. There used to be seven places to get your nails done within two miles of my house. Now there are four. The customers from the other places will gravitate to the survivors. The survivors are stronger.

Yet there's another reason that shows more evidence of the Darwinian process at work, which will strengthen business owners like me once this recession turns around. It's a new and healthy disbelief in the establishment.

Oh, we saw those big-time CEOs of big-time auto companies take first class jets and stay in fancy hotels while asking for bailouts without a financial plan. And we've seen more such CEOs of big-time financial institutions with no explanation why their billion-dollar companies vanished into thin air over a weekend. The surviving business owners who emerged from this recession discovered that those big-time guys pretending they're smart and important really don't know any more than we do. Because of this, the recession has made these small business survivors more wary, guarded, cautious, conservative, confident, and stronger. Darwin would agree. Maybe we know more than we think. We're here. They're not.

The final reason why we're stronger now that this recession is over has to do with fundamentals. There's a newfound wariness in selling too much into one industry or relying on just one customer. There's a recent understanding of the importance of putting a few bucks away to ride out the ups and downs. There's a new appreciation for those accountants and consultants who warned us against building up too much overhead. There's a respect for the guy who didn't upgrade his computer systems just because some propeller head told him it would "be cool to do it." We saw those auto dealers and parts suppliers crumble as their industry was shaken. We watched those companies—with too much payroll, too many facilities, too-high rents, too much useless yet expensive technology— go down.

Because, when things turned south, business owners that lived through the downturn learned to be flexible. They will have learned how important it is to be able to cut prices or add more value to their offerings, because that's what customers wanted most of all. Wal-Mart and McDonald's and all the other low-cost/high-value companies understand this. Let's hope we'll never forget this lesson. Darwin would not want it any other way.

Recession Lesson 2: The Last Crisis Was a Boon for Some Small Businesses

Most small business owners, like me, can find some hopeful signs coming out of the financial nightmare that gripped this country. I'm talking about people who have been running businesses for a while, who employ people, and have customers. It's those established business owners who will see some benefits of this mess in future years. Here are a few reasons why.

We're about to have a better relationship with our banker than we've ever had.

Know how over the past few years banks have been ignoring us, chasing the big money? Remember when we used to get tickets to the ball game or taken out for a round of golf? It's back. Suddenly, those boring little local banks that lent money to small businesses with actual assets are looking pretty smart right now. Surviving institutions, their egos bruised and their credibility in ruins, want to be boring too. Look for a change in the way the banking industry operates. A little more humble. A lot more relationship. They've taken their eye off the ball, chasing those subprime mortgage pots of gold for too long. It's time to welcome a resurgence of the old fashioned banker. Our businesses will be better off because of it.

We'll forget about stocks for a while.

In the good old days of the Dow 14,000, it looked as if the sky was the limit. Hey, why not take that extra cash and invest it on Wall Street? Who cares about that peeling paint and underpaid manager? We don't need those product enhancements or new machinery. There's money to be made with that guy from Merrill Lynch!

Well, we've all been burned a bit. And that guy from Merrill Lynch is serving me pepperoni slices at the local pizza shop. We've learned a lesson. Maybe investing our excess funds in better equipment or our people is a better long-term investment than that mutual fund holding securities in a company I've never heard of. Now that the stock market has lost its shine, business owners and managers will start doing what we should have been doing all along. Reinvesting our money into our own companies is good for…us.

We'll rediscover our balance sheets.

Those bankers I mentioned before? Well, not only will they be paying more attention to us but they'll be paying even more attention to our financial statements. Those quarterly numbers and covenants from our loan agreements that they always seemed to overlook because they were too busy chasing those other big deals? They'll be looking at them now, trust me. Get ready to face some scrutiny. The last thing these bankers want is to get burned again.

But this is not a bad thing; it's a good thing. Quarterly financial statements and debt covenants are not a punishment. They're great metrics to help evaluate the profitability and value of a company. Shouldn't we have been paying close attention to all of this in the first place? It'll be more difficult to get credit for those companies that probably shouldn't be getting credit in the first place. There will be better financing opportunities for those companies that deserve it. It's time that we all get more disciplined. More prudent. More focused. Our bankers are now going to require this. And for good reason.

We'll raise our prices.

Why? It isn't just to keep up with inflation (which is probably going to happen from all the money flooding the system by the Fed). It is because all of those idiot competitors of ours, without financing and facing a slow economy, are choking on the fumes of their sputtering businesses. Suddenly, not showing up to jobs and doing shoddy work means something.

We knew they didn't know what they were doing. And now they're living down to their expectations. We've always known we do better work. And that our prices are worth it. But how can we possibly prove it when some knucklehead with half the experience is also charging 20% less? Watch them fall. And watch our prices rise. Recessions and financial crises have a way of pruning the fat from the economy. The strong survive, and rise we shall.

We'll have a little more respect for regulation.

Small business owners, like myself, are loath to give the government credit for anything. We hate red tape and all the things that bureaucracy can to do to a capitalist society. We don't like big government spending or large tax increases. It's just part of our DNA.

But even this right-of-center writer has to have a little respect. It's not 1929 or 1907. There's the Fed and the Treasury and the Securities & Exchange Commission. No, they're not perfect. But they've kept the system going at a time when, historically, it would have imploded spectacularly.

They've so far coordinated pretty well with foreign central banks. Congress raised the FDIC insurance coverage on our bank accounts. They stepped in to do something to right all those bad loans. And they're making it easier for Warren Buffett to make even more money. I'm happy for Warren Buffett, too—he seems like a really nice guy. They have proven to me that there needs to be a role for regulation in a capitalist society.

We'll grab some space, too.

One day the newspapers are crying because real estate is so high no one can afford it. The next day they're crying because prices have dropped.

Well, we're not crying. The bursting real estate bubble means that we can finally, finally, finally buy that building or rent that space at a reasonable price. Not that overly inflated fairy tale of a price we were offered just a year ago. Now's the time to look for bargains. And the bankers will loan us the money...after they've protected us both by doing the appropriate amount of due diligence.

It's been tough going for a lot of small business owners while the economy rights itself. If we're lucky, we've still got a few bucks in the bank and a few good employees working hard for us. With that combination, smart business owners, and their newfound banking friends, have taken advantage of this financial crisis and turned it into a long-term success.

The Case For Not Having A Board

Received wisdom says entrepreneurs--control freaks by nature--should assemble a trusted, independent board of directors who can lend valuable strategic perspective; connect business owners with vendors, partners and lenders; and help craft effective compensation structures and internal controls.

I have the honor of sitting on a few boards, and working with those who sit on them, and I've got news for you: Boards aren't all they're cracked up to be.

"People told me a good board would help me manage my business--bad advice," says one of my clients who prefers not to be named here. "It's been nothing but a large pain in the butt."

You'd think Peter Gleason, managing director of the National Association of Corporate Directors would beg to differ about the merits of having a board. "It's definitely not for everyone," he admits.

Publicly held companies are required to have a board of directories, ostensibly to protect the rights of shareholders. (We know how that has worked out for the likes of Enron, Merrill Lynch and host of errant names in recent years.) Privately held firms often have no such mandate (some states require it), though they are being encouraged to join the band.

If you're going to have a board, get ready to open your books, strategy and management to serious scrutiny. If we make the time to be at your company and listen to your problems, we expect you to make the same commitment. That means giving us the information well in advance so that we have the time to review it. And if we make suggestions, we don't expect to be blown off.

"If you're not willing to listen to input from other experts or peers, then don't bother wasting everyone's time," says Gleason. "That's why directors resign."

Oh, we expect to be paid for the effort too. In cash. And perhaps a bit of equity. The largest public companies pay their board members up to $200,000 a year. Those at a smaller, privately held company might settle for 5% to 10% of that amount, depending on the size of the operation. And don't forget to pick up the tab for the directors and officers insurance too.

Not getting what you're paying for and want to give us the boot? You'll need a majority vote among the remaining board members to do it, so you'd best choose wisely. (Hint: Bringing on people you actually like helps a lot.)

If you want the benefits of a brain trust without the attendant hassles, you may want to create a board of advisors. Directors and advisors can perform the same functions, while advisors don't require the same legal standing and compensation.

SBDC's Are A-OK With Me

I had a great college experience recently that I'd like to share.

No, it didn't involve beer pong, foosball, hazing of freshmen or being ignored by countless girls. That was my college experience over 20 years ago. This one involved real live intelligent students (yes, there are some of those around), responsible faculty and a small business client of mine.

My client, Alan, participated in a program with a Small Business Development Center. He got some amazing advice and paid ... nothing. Businesspeople: take note.

The SBDC program is sponsored by the Small Business Administration. Go to www.sba.gov and look for the link to SBA Resource partners at the bottom of their page. Each state has a main office and numerous regional centers. For example, there are 10 centers in Pennsylvania and over 30 in Florida alone. In Philly, I personally like the one at the Wharton School because I feel like I'm really smart when I visit.

So how did Alan make use of the SBDC? What follows is his story, with just a few tiny facts changed so I don't give away any confidential information.

Alan's company sells a small device called the Cell Phone Detonator. The device helps concerned citizens perform a very useful service. When aimed at a person talking loudly on a cell phone in an inappropriate place, the Cell Phone Detonator ignites that person's phone, causing it to explode. As you can imagine, the device has been selling like hotcakes. Alan's company has won accolades from many adoring customers.

Now Alan wants to expand into a whole new market with a whole new product line called the Ring-Tone Detonator. This innovative and exciting new product can be pre-programmed with a database of the most annoying ring tones. The Ring-Tone Detonator is alerted whenever one of those annoying ring tones are played within a 100-foot radius and automatically sends a signal to the offending phone again, causing it to spontaneously combust.

Alan thinks his Ring-Tone Detonator will be a hit. Before making the investment he went to the SBDC for help. "How can I be sure there's a market for this product?" Alan asked earnestly. "How do I know it's a worthwhile investment for me?"

The students, both grads and undergrads, went to work. They researched the exploding cell phone marketplace. They conducted surveys. They interviewed industry professionals and people that ride subways. They even tested the product on a sample group of seventh-grade Jonas Brothers' fans (the results were very satisfactory). And then they put together a report for Alan.

Not surprisingly, they found that there are millions of people who would genuinely enjoy watching both the owner of a phone with an annoying ring tone, and the phone itself, go up in flames. Those particularly nauseating pre-programmed ring tones with kids voices telling the owner to "pick up the phone mommy, pick up the phone mommy" topped the list. Alan's thinking of another product to make the kids explode too.

So for free, the students at the SBDC helped Alan make a key marketing decision. They did a report that would have cost Alan thousands if he had gone to an outside consulting

299

firm.

SBDCs are generally associated with universities. They want to give their business students a shot at helping business owners make decisions. Sure they're younger and have little or no real world experience. But an academic analysis of any problem, be it marketing, whether to sell your business, buy another company, restructure or hire a key manager can be very helpful. And the price is certainly right.

Smart managers take free consulting when they can get it, and the SBDC program is a great source for anyone. Uh-oh, here comes Alan. I better change my ring tone from that Usher tune to something by Sinatra before something awful happens.

Tom Is Selling His Business

I admit that sometimes I live in a fantasy world. I actually think that I'm getting a buzz from lite beer. I sometimes believe that John Edwards can really talk to the dead. Or that John Edward's marriage isn't dead. Or is it the other way around? Geez, those guys kind of look alike anyway.

I have a friend named Tom who's looking to sell his equipment parts distribution business. Problem is he can't sell it. He's had more than a half dozen potential buyers and they've all offered way less than what he was looking for.

What's the problem? Tom lives in his own fantasy world. He thinks his company is worth may more than it really is. That's almost as bad as thinking two cheeseburgers at McDonalds is healthier than a Big Mac (everyone knows it's the FRIES that'll kill you).

On the outside, it looks like Tom's business isn't even so bad. He's been running it for over twenty years. It's provided him with a good income, enough to keep his three kids our of jail and even sufficient to send two of them to college. It's paid for the lease on his BMW (which, in Tom's fantasy world is a better car than a Hyundai even though we all know it's all about status).

Tom's got a good amount of cash in the bank. Granted, a little less than before the market crashed. But it's coming back. His balance sheet shows receivables at least 50% higher than his payables and no other major liabilities on the books.

He even owns the building that houses his company. So, now that he's hitting his mid-60's why can't he unload the thing and retire?

The same reasons why many penny pinching business owners find out their business is worth a lot less than they thought. They don't take care of the intangibles. And so they live in a fantasy world.

For example, after over twenty years of existence you'd think that Tom's company would have a database of its customers? Not a chance. Instead there are spreadsheets, email files, paper files, sticky notes and some bare bones information in his accounting system necessary for printing out an invoice. Snooki from The Jersey Shore is probably more organized. Tom never collected profile information about his customers. What products they bought. What products they might be interested in buying. Organizations they belong to. The lite beer they drink. Favorite sports teams.

And he certainly never did this for his prospects either. Thousands of interested customers have passed through Tom's world over the years, many of them getting quotes or callbacks from his sales guys. But was this data stored? Nope. All the information was in Tom's head. Not in a database. And if it did get filed somewhere the data was never updated. It's of little value to a buyer. Tom didn't realize this.

That's because buyers are looking for something more than just cash, receivables and hard assets. They pay extra, a lot extra, for solid intangible assets too. A complete and accurate customer database is a huge value to an incoming owner. A complete and accurate prospect database is icing on the cake. Some deals are made because of the strength of the seller's data. If Tom was more organized then he might have more reason to entice a potential buyer.

Tom also thought that once he sold his business he could wash his hands and walk away. That's almost as big a fantasy as those dopey people buying dirt from the old Veterans Stadium in Philadelphia before it was imploded and thinking it would one day be valuable. It's dirt! In a bottle! A bottle of dirt!

And without the seller staying on for a few years to ensure a successful transition, the value of a potential acquisition can quickly become dirt too. A potential buyer of a small company rarely buys that company unless they intend to bring on its existing management for a period of time. Like most companies, Tom's would fall apart if he wasn't there. This would change overnight? The minute Tom told a potential buyer that he was "outta here" any seller would turn and walk right out the door. Good penny pinchers who want to sell their companies know that the selling process continues even after the sale is made. They have to stay on for a while. It's the only way to maximize the value of their asset.

Sure, I admit to fantasizing about a lot of things. Getting rich. Sailing around the world. Having hair. But I'm kind of proud to say that I don't have fantasies about my business. Without me, it's valueless. My clients like us a lot. My employees (I think) like me a lot. But I lack long term contracts with any of them. To a potential buyer, this is a big problem.

Tom thinks he's got a long term relationships with his customers. He thinks his employees will stay on forever after he's gone. But that's a fantasy. He's a distributor. He has no service contracts. No commitments. No employment agreements. A customer can jump to one of his competitors tomorrow without recourse. A key employee can quit next week without any further thought. Accounting firms are easy to value because most clients have long term engagements that can be easily forecasted. It's kind of a pain to leave your accountant. So there's a predictable future revenue stream. Tom does not have this. He thinks he does. But it's a fantasy.

The world is full of people who like to fantasize. Barack

Obama fantasizes that Republicans and Democrats will actually one day work together. My friend in New York fantasizes that the Mets may have a winning season this year. Ashton Kutcher fantasizes that people actually cares what he tweets.

And some people, like Tom, fantasize that their business is worth way more than it really is. Time for a wake up call.

Profiting From Healthcare

The Affordable Care Act is real. It's law. And it's moving forward. That's a fact. And, while so many businesses are figuring out how this change in health insurance law will affect them, many others are doing what Americans do best: figuring out how to profit. Because that's what smart entrepreneurs do. Other than election day, they put aside their emotions, tuck their political leanings aside, and work within the current environment to maximize their profits. Politics are important, of course. But a business owner has payroll to meet, a family to feed and partners, customers and suppliers who rely on his (or her) business.

So you may or may not support our President. You may or may not agree with healthcare reform. In the meantime, consider these few ideas to profit from it. Because I promise you, your competitors are doing just that.

Reduce your tax expense. If you're employing less than 25 full time people whose average salary is less than $50,000 per year then you're entitled to a tax credit for a portion of what you're paying every year in health insurance. The maximum credit (50%) is available for those employing less than 10 full time people making an average of $25,000 per year. But there's still a few bucks for grabs, so grab it.

Do business with the state exchanges. By January 1, 2014 all of my children are required to have moved out of my house and all states are required to have exchanges setup so that individuals and companies who choose to do so can purchase their health insurance. Many states have delayed action pending the outcome of the Supreme Court decision. Now it's on. Does your firm provide web programming or design services? Are there opportunities for development work? Any interest in taking on college age boarders? You bet there are. Contact your state (or me) now...many of us need the help.

Get rid of your insurance. When the fabled state exchanges are up and running you'll be encouraged to let your employees get their insurance there. What is this dark magic and how will it work? You'll be required to maintain a "qualified" plan and if you don't you'll be penalized...I'm sorry...taxed (according to the Supreme Court). So why fight City Hall? Having your employees to purchase their health insurance from the state exchanges, even with some reimbursement from you, may still be cheaper in the long run. For sure it'll be easier to budget your health insurance costs and it will certainly eliminate the internal cost (not to mention the complaints) of your office manager administrating all the forms and communications required by the current plan you have.

Take advantage of pre-existing conditions. No one can deny that Batman is a nutcase. But what business wouldn't want to hire him for overnight security, am I right? Hiring a guy with deep psychological issues like Batman in the past wasn't easy. But now anyone with a pre-existing condition will soon be able to move from job to job and their insurance companies are not allowed to drop or deny coverage. So if you're looking for that key person with that special skill (or a really cool Batarang) who you couldn't hire before because he or she would lose coverage...now you can. And if you're an employee looking to switch jobs or start your own business and couldn't before...now you can.

You're in the right place if you're in biotech. In recent years it's been the web, mobile and Betty White who have received all the attention. But with 34 million more people entering the market many experts predict the emergence of new stars: companies developing new medical and biotechnology products. A science writer reported back on the bill's original passage "...there are two small bits in the Patient Protection and Affordable Care Act that are immediately relevant and timely for the biotechnology industry. One provides tax breaks for smaller biotechnology companies, while the other simplifies some aspects of the regulatory landscape and adds some complicated wrinkles." Another biotech boom?

Jump into Electronic Health Records (EHR). With so many more new customers entering into the insurance market, the activity around EHRs will no doubt be heating up. Buoyed by a $20 billion investment as part of the 2009 stimulus, I once wrote elsewhere how the progress towards creating EHRs has taken a large leap forward. Look for even more opportunities if you can help integrate existing software systems, write code to improve user interfaces, play a professional sport without relying on performance enhancing drugs, sell and customize tablets and handhelds for doctors to use or provide training and consulting.

Consider a little consulting or speaking. Speaking of consulting, and speaking of speaking, there's going to be plenty of need for all of that over the next few years. Just about every client I know is confused by how this law will affect their business. They need help. If you're an expert (or can sing and dance a little) there are plenty of opportunities to help small, medium and large sized companies navigate their way around the law. And plenty of other opportunities to speak to groups about the plan's effects. Do we stick with our existing plan? Do we drop coverage and send our people to the state exchanges? What are the state exchanges? When will Betty White host SNL again? See what I mean?

Provide indirect services to the healthcare industry. Hospitals and other healthcare providers have been applauding the Supreme Court ruling. Why? Because, like it or not, the Act adds millions of new customers to the markets and provides a way for insurance companies to pay for their services. That can only mean more business for the healthcare industry. To me, that means growth. Maybe you're not in the healthcare business. But that doesn't mean that the healthcare business can't do business with your business. Growing organizations will still need help with office supplies, technology, waste removal, capital equipment...even landscaping. Smart business owners I know hitch themselves with growing industries and promote their services to them. This way they grow together.

Keep an eye on new markets. The Act will certainly be opening up new markets where you can sell your products and services. For example, one acupuncturist is on pins and needles (get it?) because "....by 2014, Section 3502 of President Obama's healthcare reform could mandate the Bureau of Health Statistics to formally recognize acupuncture as a profession, opening the door to Medicare coverage for acupuncture, serving our growing elderly population, as well as providing it as an option for millions of low- and middle-income Americans in need of care."

Help wanted: payments and process consulting. Are you an expert in electronic payments, mobile technology or provide business process consulting? Consider these opportunities: Section 3021 of the legislation establishes the Center for Medicare and Medicaid Innovation whose purpose will be to innovate payment and delivery of services to patients. Section 6301 provides funding for a new patient-centered Outcomes Research Institute whose purpose is to help government, employers, consumers and private insurers determine which treatment/procedures offer good value for their cost. Now there are a couple of organizations that could use your consulting help if you've got the expertise.

Become an auditor. It's great that healthcare coverage will be provided for all, including the 34 million or so who don't currently have it. And it's great that the government will penalize...I'm sorry....tax those that don't get health insurance. But who's going to enforce that? If it's a tax, then it must be the IRS. And if people couldn't afford health insurance before, there's a good chance that many won't be able to afford it no matter what the penalty...I'm sorry...tax is. Next up: here come the auditors! Plenty of experts feel that there will be a significant need for auditors to help enforce this law. Maybe your firm can help provide these services?

The country will survive healthcare reform. Who knows? We may even be better off from it. Two things about the legislation are for sure: some smart entrepreneurs will profit from the changes in the law. And Betty White will probably use it to figure out a way to live another hundred years.

Uncertainty

I was in Washington and met with two Congressmen who sit on the House Committee for Small Business. When I asked them each what they're hearing most when they speak to small businesses around the country I received the same answer from both.

Uncertainty.

"Small businesses are uncertain about so many things today," said Rep. Mark Hanna (R-NY). "They're uncertain about taxes, government regulation, our national debt, healthcare reform. I hear this all the time."

He's right. I hear it too. From my clients. From my readers. From the people at events where I speak. The economy isn't growing and the media reports that it's because so many business people are uncertain. And this sentiment isn't exclusive to small business. Big businesses, like Nissan and FedEx are using "uncertainty" to explain their own financial challenges. "Uncertainty" has defined the economy and is the big issue in this election year.

I can relate. I'm very uncertain too. For example, I'm uncertain whether I can last the entire summer with my three teenage kids in the house without killing at least one of them. I'm uncertain about whether I should commit time to watching "Game of Thrones" because my tech guy says it's the best TV show he ever watched (I'm uncertain on this because my tech guy is also a regular attendee of the Comic-Con conferences). As I write this, I'm kind of uncertain about whether the guy sitting next to me in seat 7B has bathed anytime within the past week. So yes, I'm uncertain about a lot of things.

And, of course, I'm uncertain about my business. And the economy. And the political environment. And world peace. And disease. And the weather. And why my Coke kind of tastes like my flight attendant's thumb. And whether an asteroid will hit the earth. And whether Peggy will return for another season on Mad Men. Like so many others, I use uncertainty as an excuse for why my business hasn't been growing. I blame our "uncertain" economy and nod my head in agreement when my colleagues and clients curse the world around them.

But wait just a second. Since when have things ever been certain? Since when do people know for sure what's going to happen in the future? At what point did smart, independent, risk-taking small business people suddenly start blaming all of their problems on uncertainty? Isn't uncertainty an historical part of running any business? A big part?

Let's say you were running your business anytime in the past forty years or so. What, things were less certain in the early '60's? With the threat of nuclear war, the steel industry fixing prices, escalation in Vietnam, soldiers shooting at college students, politicians murdered almost nightly, black people hosed in the streets, massive protests, the Carpenters music playing everywhere? Those were uncertain times. And did things really get better in the '70's, with high inflation, long gas lines, terrorism, a President who was forced to resign, Sonny & Cher? Were things any less certain under the reigns of Reagan, Bush, Clinton and Bush? Exactly what was done with that cigar in the oval office anyway?

311

Of course things are never certain. There's never been an easy time to run a small business. Is this a surprise? For thousands of years business people, industrialists and shopkeepers have lived under the threat of excessive government taxation, military conscription, plague, bad teeth, over-cooked mutton and wars that killed our children and depleted our resources. Like any fan attending this summer's Euro games, we've suffered invasions, looting and rioting. We've seen interest rates and inflation skyrocket, stock markets collapse and our currency lose its value almost overnight. Politicians and leaders make promises…and then change their minds a year later.

And yet we, as Americans, continue to complain about "uncertainty." This, at the same moment of history where a dictator has assumed the leadership of Russia (again), punishing those that speak out against his government, a socialist has been elected in France as neighboring countries teeter in the face of economic collapse from spending too much on social programs, civil wars have devastated Syria and Libya and the world is entrusting the British, yes the British, to run this year's Olympic games. By comparison, our country looks downright stable.

Maybe the reason I hear so much about "uncertainty" is related to the people I'm hearing it from. Losing your job as a result of the recent recession can make anyone feel uncertain. And, like so many of those who find themselves running a small business for the first time to generate income, they're finding that it's a cold, hard world out here. Here's certainty: having a job with health benefits and a retirement plan plus a nice boss, a yummy choice of organic coffees in the break room and "casual Fridays." Here's uncertainty: getting up at six in the morning, enduring abuse from the few customers you're managed to scrape together, banging your head trying to find that mysterious subcontractor who promised to deliver

312

by today, begging for money owed you from work done three months ago, tossing and turning all night wondering if that big project will finish on time and if it doesn't where are you going to get the money to pay the suppliers you owe. Running a small business can be scary, risky, stressful and most of all uncertain. Methinks there are many new entrepreneurs finding this out right now and they're the ones who are yelling the loudest.

I don't hear the word "uncertainty" from true blue entrepreneurs. You know who I'm talking about. This publication reports on them every day. These are the ones who are getting financing, creating new technologies, making a killing on Wall Street, snapping up competitors who lose their mojo, buying used equipment for a song or partnering with sketchy people in China or East Africa because there's money to be made. Are these people uncertain? Of course they are. But they love it! Because that's their thrill. That's how they make money. Business, all business, is a bet. A gamble. Because they are true business people they understand the concept of risk and reward. The more uncertainty, the more reward for the right bet.

And I don't hear the word "uncertainty" from the typical small business owner. The 20 million of us who are running tech firms, baking pizzas, changing oil, mowing lawns, buying high, selling low. I hear words like "slow", "terrible", "frustrating" and a host of other profanities for which my editors would lose their jobs if they allowed them to be displayed here.

There are plenty of reports of how corporations are sitting on a mountain of cash but unwilling to spend because of uncertain times. Actually, business investment has been up over the past few years. I talk to many business executives and uncertainty really has nothing to do with why they're not spending more. These guys are not spending this money because there's nothing to spend it on. The economy is not growing and neither are their customers. They're eking out profits by cutting costs and keeping employee numbers low. There's no need to stock up on inventory when demand is slow. They don't have to build new buildings when they have less employees. They don't need more equipment when they're able to produce all they need with the equipment they have. This is not uncertainty. It's choice. These guys are quite happy to take the risk. They get that nothing's certain. They understand that any investment they make may not pay off.

Will higher taxes bring on another recession? Will planned cuts in government spending do the same? Will our national debt bankrupt us? Will healthcare reform, in all or in part, have an impact on our economy? Will the Fed's money policies fuel inflation and higher interest rates? Will our dollar regain or lose strength? Will Rielle Hunter and John Edwards ever get back together again?

These are big questions. But they are not new questions. These are the same issues that businesses have been facing since Caesar. It's just that today there are no gladiator fights or orgies. Successful entrepreneurs understand this and thrive. The rest of us just complain.

Conclusion:
Homage To Jim and Rich

I've lived in the same neighborhood outside of Philadelphia for over ten years now. And it's time to pay homage to two business owners that really get it: Jim and Rich.

Are you thinking of starting your own business? Do you already own a business and wish you could be doing better? Forget about the experts and the pundits. Stop reading the columns and the articles. Ignore the advice from the talking heads and the geniuses. The two guys to learn from are Jim and Rich.

Jim owns Township Cleaners and Rich owns a gas station/repair shop directly across Montgomery Avenue called Wark's Auto. These are their real names. These are their real businesses.

Neither of these guys are super-millionaires. They're not building empires. They don't plan to take their companies public. I don't even know how profitable they are. But, trust me, they're profitable. I'm sure, like the rest of us, they both wish they could be making more money. I'm sure they'd like to retire one day and sit on a beach. Are they happy? I don't know them well enough to say. But I do know they're realistic. They work hard. And smart. And they show up every day.

And therein lies the first lesson for fledgling startups. Show up. Early. And stay late. Both Township Cleaners and Wark's Auto cater to people who need to drop off their dry cleaning before their workday starts and fill up their gas tanks on their way home from a dinner meeting. These guys always seem open. They start the day near dawn. They stay open late. They're open on the weekends.

And they always seem to be there. When I bring in my shirts Jim takes them from me. When I pay for gas I see Rich in the shop. They keep a close, close eye on things. Maybe they're micro-managing too much, I don't know. But nothing seems to get by them. They're on top of every customer, every job. They don't seem to delegate a whole lot. Which means that neither of them probably have the skill set to manage a large group of people. But that's OK. They seem to know their own limitations. So instead they manage the hell out of their small group of employees. They roll up their sleeves and sew, press, change valves and replace carburetors.

And their employees seem to have no problem with that. In fact, during the ten years I've been living here I keep seeing the same faces again and again at Township Cleaners and Wark's. During this same time I've managed technology projects at much larger corporations and routinely deal with a revolving door of employees who have come and gone from these companies whether at will or involuntarily. But at Township Cleaners and Wark's the people have pretty much remained the same. Why? Are the benefits superior? Are their salaries higher? Probably not. It's because these people recognize a devoted, serious business owner and have decided to hitch their wagons along with him. For better or worse. And from what I can tell, it's better.

Another thing I like about their businesses? They bend over backwards for their customers. First of all, they're fast at what they do. They value our time. Jim runs his little dry cleaning shop like a machine. Rarely am I in there for more than 5 minutes. I've dropped off my car at all hours of the day for Warks to repair and then come home to find it has been delivered back to my house, keys in the glove compartment. I ask Jim to put a rush on a sport jacket and he says "no problem." My wife asks Rich if she can run over to have a front headlight replaced and he says "no problem." There are too many people in this world who give us problems. Township Cleaners and Warks are not among them.

Oh, by the way: they're not cheap either. I haven't compared dry cleaning rates but I'm betting that Jim charges more than a competitor in a less affluent area may charge. Same with Rich. But they prove that you get what you pay for. There's a value we put on our time, convenience and great service. They get that. They charge. But they execute on this promise. Maybe they could get more customers if they charge less. I don't know. But they're certainly keeping the customers they have at their current rates.

One final thing I like about both these companies: they use technology well. For too long business owners and managers have been inundated by stupid technology recommendations from stupid technology people. Jim and Rich don't have websites. They don't do social networking for their businesses. They don't have complex bar-coding systems. They have just the right mix of software, hardware, cash registers, credit card machines and old fashioned paper for them to get their work done efficiently. Jim's got every item in his shop entered into his system, yet half the time he seems to find my stuff without even referring to it. Rich's got the basic self-serve gas pumps and tools in his shop that helps his mechanics get their work done. But nothing more than that. They don't need it. They get it.

Aren't these guys boring? Isn't it all so mundane? Well, that's what running a small business is all about. Sure, it's fun to read about those companies that start with nothing and become titans in their industry. And it's entertaining to hear about those entrepreneurs who buy, sell, fall down, get up, expand, lose money and make money. They are gamblers and risk takers. They make great stories. But there are more than

317

20 million small businesses in this country. And many of them are boring, average, normal business owners like Jim and Rich. Thank God for that.

19362358R00192

Made in the USA
Charleston, SC
19 May 2013